THE
13 POWER MOVES OF
DARK
PSYCHOLOGY

Ninth Bridge is an imprint of BenBella Books, Inc.
8080 N. Central Expressway
Suite 1700
Dallas, TX 75206
benbellabooks.com
Send feedback to feedback@benbellabooks.com

BenBella is a federally registered trademark.

Printed in the United States of America

10 9 8 7 6 5 4 3 2 1

Library of Congress Control Number: 2025007641
ISBN 9781637746981 (paper over board)
ISBN 9781637746998 (electronic)

Design by Joanna Williams
Composition by Twozdai Hulse
Cover illustration used under license from Shutterstock.com

**Special discounts for bulk sales are available. Please contact
bulkorders@benbellabooks.com.**

THE
13 POWER MOVES OF
DARK
PSYCHOLOGY

LEARN THE TRICKS TO
PROTECT YOURSELF
FROM ABUSE
AND COVERTLY
INFLUENCE ANYONE

LENA SISCO

NINTH
BRIDGE
—BOOKS—

CONT

Foreword 7

Introduction to Dark Psychology 11

1 • DARK PSYCHOLOGY DECODED 15

2 • PERSUASION VS. DARK PSYCHOLOGY 29

3 • MOST LIKELY TO DECEIVE: PEOPLE
AND PERSONALITY DISORDERS 35

4 • DECEITFUL GAMES AND TOXIC LIES 45

5 • LOVE AND DARK PSYCHOLOGY 65

6 • FAMILY AND DARK PSYCHOLOGY 81

7 • THE WORKPLACE AND DARK
PSYCHOLOGY 89

8 • 13 POWER MOVES TO FIGHT BACK 107

ENTS

9 • **#1 TRUST YOUR GUT AND #2 INVESTIGATE IT** 113

10 • **#3 HOLD THEM ACCOUNTABLE AND #4 AVOID FLYTRAPS** 141

11 • **#5 COVERTLY INFLUENCE MANIPULATORS** 161

12 • **#6 CONTROL THE NARRATIVE** 173

13 • **#7 STEP INTO YOUR POWER, #8 TURN THE TABLES, AND #9 SET BOUNDARIES** 197

14 • **#10 ADD SOME DISTANCE OR #11 WALK AWAY** 219

15 • **#12 GET SUPPORT AND #13 BE RESILIENT** . . 225

VICTIM RESOURCES 236

ACKNOWLEDGMENTS 237

SOURCES 239

FOREWORD

AS A FORMER FBI SPECIAL AGENT WITH OVER TWENTY-TWO YEARS OF SERVICE, I dedicated my career to understanding the intricate and often perilous manifestations of human behavior. During my time as chief of the counterintelligence behavioral analysis team for the FBI, I conducted countless behavioral assessments, always with a singular mission: to protect our nation from those who would seek to exploit and destroy us. In this pursuit, I witnessed firsthand the dark undercurrents of human psychology—how individuals manipulate, deceive, and undermine, often with devastating consequences.

It is from this vantage point that I introduce my good friend and esteemed colleague, Lena Sisco, whose book *The 13 Power Moves of Dark Psychology* is an essential guide for anyone seeking to navigate the treacherous waters of human interaction. Lena's extensive experience as a Navy human intelligence officer and military interrogator has equipped her with unique insights into the mechanics of manipulation and deceit. This book distills her years of practical experience into actionable strategies that anyone can apply to protect themselves and their loved ones.

The purpose of this book is clear and crucial. In a world where trust is often misplaced and intentions can be veiled, understanding dark psychology is not just an academic pursuit; it is a necessary skill for safeguarding our well-being. Lena adeptly outlines how dark psychology manifests in everyday life—from subtle manipulations in personal relationships to the coercive tactics employed in professional environments. This book will resonate with anyone who has ever felt the sting of betrayal or the unease of being manipulated.

Reflecting on my career, I recall a particularly striking case involving a highly skilled con artist whose life parallels that of Frank Abagnale, the infamous figure depicted in *Catch Me If You Can*. This individual had once served as a CIA officer but left the agency under dubious circumstances. He then morphed into a masterful con artist, seamlessly adopting various identities—lawyer, pastor, political operative—and practicing the art of deception with an ease that left us in awe.

Our investigation brought us face-to-face with a man who not only boasted a high IQ, but also possessed the chilling ability to manipulate those around him with charm and charisma. During our interviews, it became clear that he thrived on the attention and admiration he received from others. The challenge was formidable; traditional rapport-building techniques—designed for individuals with normal psychological profiles—would be utterly ineffective against someone of his caliber.

This con artist was a true psychopath, fully aware of how to exploit the emotions and vulnerabilities of those around him. In one particular instance, he attempted to use our own insecurities against us, weaving a narrative that flattered our egos while simultaneously trying to intimidate us into submission. He tried to create a power dynamic, playing on our fears of inadequacy and doubt. Recognizing his tactics was essential; we had to remain sharp and strategic in our approach.

To counter his manipulation, we employed our own form of dark psychology, appealing to his grandiosity and need for validation. We framed our questions in a way that challenged his self-image, suggesting he could never truly compare to a master con artist like Frank Abagnale. The moment we mentioned Abagnale's name, we saw a flicker of anger in his eyes; he felt the need to prove himself. This pivotal moment turned the tide of our interaction. To assert his superiority and silence our doubts, he began to divulge the details of his operations and where he had stashed millions of dollars in stolen money, proud to have exceeded anything Abagnale had ever achieved.

Through careful elicitation techniques, we expressed disbelief in his claims. By doing so, we struck a nerve; he was compelled to prove us wrong. This intricate dance of manipulation and countermanipulation ultimately led to his confession and the recovery of the stolen assets, a testament to the power of understanding dark psychology.

Dark psychology, as Lena explains, refers to the strategic use of psychological tactics to exploit, control, and harm others. It's a pervasive force in our lives, often lurking in the shadows of our interactions—be it in the workplace, at home, or even in casual social settings. The implications are significant: Understanding dark psychology is not merely about identifying deceitful individuals but about empowering yourself with the tools to navigate these dynamics safely and effectively.

This book is for everyone—those embarking on new relationships, business leaders striving to make informed decisions, individuals recovering from manipulation, or anyone who simply wishes to fortify their defenses against psychological abuse. Lena's profound insights and actionable strategies provide readers with a comprehensive toolkit to recognize and combat manipulation, ensuring that they can reclaim their power and maintain their confidence.

In *The 13 Power Moves of Dark Psychology*, Lena distills her extensive knowledge into thirteen fundamental principles that serve as golden keys to unlock a safer, more fulfilling existence. These power moves will prepare you to confront manipulative behaviors head-on, allow you to build healthier relationships, and empower you to create unbreakable alliances in your personal and professional life.

As you engage with this book, I encourage you to reflect on your own experiences with manipulation and the lessons they hold. Embrace Lena's insights as a transformative guide, equipping you with knowledge that can shield you from harm and foster resilience against psychological threats.

In life, we are continually confronted with opposing forces—light and dark, trust and betrayal, confidence and vulnerability. It is through understanding these dynamics that we can cultivate healthy relationships and forge strong alliances. I urge you to approach this book with an open heart and mind, ready to enhance your skills and knowledge. Armed with Lena Sisco's wisdom, you have the potential to navigate the complexities of human interaction with confidence and clarity and nurture the kind of bonds that protect our well-being and enhance our lives.

Welcome to a journey of empowerment through understanding. Your path to psychological safety begins here.

—Robin Dreeke
Former FBI agent and Chief of the FBI Behavioral Analysis Program, author of *Unbreakable Alliances*

INTRODUCTION

WE ALL WANT TO BELIEVE IN THE GOOD IN PEOPLE.
It's natural to trust, to think those around us have our best interests at heart. But the truth is that everyone has a darker side. Ignoring it leaves us wide open to the schemes of those who operate from their worst impulses, manipulating others to take what they want—whether it's their money, confidence, or sense of control. After spending over two decades studying human behavior, I can assure you that those untrustworthy people are out there, so you should know how to spot them. My background as a naval human intelligence officer and military interrogator has given me unique insights into how people lie, deceive, and manipulate. In *The 13 Power Moves of Dark Psychology*, my mission is to share everything I've learned to help you protect yourself from people who use psychological manipulation for their own gain and who intend to cause harm to others.

SO WHAT IS DARK PSYCHOLOGY?

Dark psychology is the strategic use of psychological tactics to exploit, control, and harm others. This might sound dramatic, but you've likely already encountered it in your life. It could be sitting right next to you at work, smiling at you from across a dinner table, or even lurking in the messages on your dating app. Those who weaponize it are often subtle, even charming, as they turn everyday interactions into power plays designed to make you doubt yourself, give in to their demands, or hand over control.

Some personalities are more prone to these behaviors. People with traits from the "Dark Triad"—narcissism, Machiavellianism, and psychopathy—often operate without guilt or shame. Their moral compass is broken, and they're skilled at hiding it. You might even admire their confidence or charisma. That's the tricky part. We tend to trust people who seem sure of themselves, but confidence isn't always a sign of good intentions. Falling for their tricks doesn't mean you're naïve. These individuals are experts at creating smokescreens. Even the sharpest minds can be deceived. But recognizing the tactics they use—before they take root in your life—is the key to staying safe.

Encountering dark psychology doesn't necessarily mean you'll find yourself trapped in some dramatic, life-altering scenario. This does not always play out like a made-for-TV movie. It can start or even persist on a smaller scale. Maybe you've noticed subtle red flags already—a partner constantly shifting blame, a friend who manipulates through guilt, or a boss who demands too much for too little. If any of this sounds familiar, you're not alone. This book is for anyone who wants to sharpen their instincts to protect themselves from those who use psychological tricks to take advantage. But it's especially useful for those who are:

- Navigating a new relationship, personal or professional, and need to know whom to trust
- Running a business and want to avoid being manipulated into bad decisions
- Trying to recover from being scammed, lied to, or emotionally manipulated

Think of the moments in your own life when you've felt manipulated. Maybe you had a colleague who conveniently "forgot" to finish tasks, or pushed their work onto your plate. Perhaps it was a romantic partner who always seemed to take more than they gave, leaving you feeling used. You may have had roommates or in-laws who expected you to cater to their every whim, leaving you drained and frustrated. This is dark psychology creeping into your life, slowly chipping away at your confidence and control. The longer it goes unchecked, the more power these individuals gain.

HOW THIS BOOK CAN HELP YOU

This book isn't just about identifying those who seek to manipulate you. It's about empowering you with tools and strategies to protect yourself, to push back when needed, and to regain control of your life. Dealing with manipulative people can feel like playing a high-stakes mental chess game. The key is to stay sharp, keep your emotions in check, and know the right moves to make. Once you understand the workings of dark psychology and learn to use the thirteen power moves I'll share with you, you'll be able to take action to protect yourself—whether it's from a manipulative boss, a narcissistic partner, or a toxic friend. My goal is for you to walk away from this book with a clear sense of how to defend your mental and emotional space while keeping your power and confidence intact.

You don't have to live in fear of being deceived. Armed with the right knowledge, you can avoid unnecessary pain, reclaim your peace of mind, and steer clear of those who would seek to control or harm you.

DARK PSYCHOLOGY DECODED

BEFORE JOINING THE MILITARY, I studied archaeology at the University of Rhode Island and Brown University. I spent plenty of time learning about ancient civilizations like the Maya and Romans. If there's one thing that I learned from all that time digging through the past, it's that darkness is part of human nature. The Maya practiced brutal bloodletting rituals, sometimes even sacrificing their own people to appease their gods. The Romans? They had the gladiator games—violent spectacles that were a key part of their culture, where men fought to the death for public entertainment.

Most of us have no trouble keeping our darker impulses in check. We live by a set of morals and ethics that prevent us from lying, cheating, or exploiting others. But some people—those who are driven by darker psychological forces—don't have that same internal stop sign. They act on their desires to control, deceive, and harm others for their own pleasure and benefit, often with little or no guilt.

DARK PSYCHOLOGY: THE SOCIAL EXPERIMENT

The Stanford Prison Experiment, led by psychologist Philip Zimbardo in the 1970s, offered some insight into the kinds of conditions and environments where dark psychology rears its ugly head. He created a mock prison scenario, assigning students to play the roles of guards and prisoners. The behavior that resulted shocked everyone, even Zimbardo himself. The "guards," ordinary students, began abusing their power, humiliating and tormenting their fellow classmates, the "prisoners." It spiraled so quickly into psychological abuse that the experiment had to be shut down after just six days.

Why did some of the students devolve into the worst versions of themselves? Because the environment—a prison setting with defined power roles—allowed dark psychology to flourish. The guards weren't evil people; they were regular students who, in the right (or wrong) conditions, became capable of cruelty. The

THE MANY FACES OF DARK PSYCHOLOGY

Dark psychology refers to the harmful, manipulative behaviors that stem from certain negative personality traits that we all have (but not all of us act on). Those who use coercion and deception to get what they want, often with complete disregard for others' feelings or well-being, are the ones who do the most damage. For them, people are just tools—a means to an end.

Think of a person you know who always seems to get what they want, but leaves a trail of broken relationships behind. They probably lack empathy, have no problem taking advantage of others, and never seem to feel remorse. Maybe you've worked with someone like this, or even dated someone who left you

experiment illustrated a key point about human behavior: Given the right environment, even people who consider themselves moral might engage in unethical, harmful behavior. This wasn't just an isolated incident. Decades later, Zimbardo weighed in on the atrocities committed against prisoners at Abu Ghraib prison in 2004. The soldiers there forced the prisoners into degrading positions, committed violent acts against them, and unashamedly documented this treatment in photos and videos. Many were quick to blame the perpetrators as individually flawed, but Zimbardo saw the parallels to his own experiment. He argued that certain environments can push people toward darkness. Where unchecked power and a capacity for dehumanization coexist, even ordinary people can do terrible things.

feeling used and discarded. These behaviors often come from what psychologists call the Dark Triad—a trio of personality traits that play a central role in dark psychology: narcissism, Machiavellianism, and psychopathy. Understanding these traits and how they manifest can help you spot the warning signs before you get too close. Let's dive into each one and look at how they show up in real life.

Narcissism: More Than Just Vanity

Despite the recent flood of social media posts and books about narcissism, the term is often misused. People are quick to casually label anyone with a big ego as a narcissist, but true Narcissistic Personality Disorder (NPD) goes far beyond someone who likes themselves a little too much. Think of narcissism as a trait exhibited by a colleague or friend who constantly brags, demands praise, and gets upset when the attention shifts away from them. Chances are, you've crossed paths with someone like this. Narcissists can be quite damaging in relationships because they need constant validation. If you're in a romantic relationship with a narcissist, you'll likely find that no matter how much you give, it's never enough. They'll drain your energy and leave you feeling emotionally depleted, all the while searching for more admiration and validation from others.

But true NPD runs deeper than everyday arrogance. It's characterized by a strong sense of entitlement, a constant need for admiration, and a lack of empathy. Consider the origin of the term: the Greek myth of Narcissus, a young man who was so captivated by his own reflection that he spent his life staring at it until he eventually died. People with NPD are consumed with themselves, often to the exclusion of all else. Such people genuinely believe they are better, smarter, and more important than everyone around them. This belief drives them to behave in ways that can be incredibly toxic. They'll claim credit for other people's successes, exaggerate their accomplishments, and expect to be treated like they're special without having to earn it.

The Traits of Narcissistic Personality Disorder

To better understand how narcissists operate, let's break down some of the key traits that define Narcissistic Personality Disorder:

1. Inflated sense of self-importance: A narcissist truly believes they are superior to everyone around them. They see themselves as more successful, better-looking, and more talented. They often exaggerate their achievements and believe they are indispensable in every aspect of life, whether it's in their career, friendships, or family. If you've ever worked for a boss who takes credit for your hard work, you've probably seen this trait firsthand.

2. Entitlement: People with NPD feel they deserve special treatment simply because of who they are. They don't feel the need to earn it, and they get upset when things don't go their way. A narcissistic coworker might expect the best office or special privileges without putting in any extra effort. If you've ever been around someone who constantly complains about not getting the recognition they think they deserve, this is entitlement at work.

3. Preoccupation with fantasies: Narcissists are often consumed with fantasies of unlimited success, power, or beauty. They may spend their days imagining themselves living a life of luxury, even if their real life doesn't reflect that. This can make them seem out of touch with reality, but trying to bring them back down to earth usually only fuels their delusions.

4. Constant need for admiration: Narcissists crave admiration like others crave food or water. They need to be the center of attention and will go to great lengths to ensure the spotlight is always on them. If they don't get enough praise or attention, they may become angry or even lash out.

5. Drawn to status: Narcissists feel that they should only associate with people they consider equally special. They often seek out high-status individuals, believing that being surrounded by "important" people reflects their own importance. If they feel someone isn't on their level, they'll dismiss them as unworthy of their time. Being around important people will make them look better; being around unimportant people is of no use to them.

6. Exploitation of others: Narcissists are more than willing to take advantage of others to achieve their goals. They have no problem using people as stepping stones and often discard relationships once they've gotten what they want. Whether in the workplace or personal life, this trait can leave a wake of destruction as they move from one person to the next, always seeking something for themselves.

7. Lack of empathy: This might be the most clearly defining trait of a narcissist. They feel little to no empathy for others, which makes it easy for them to manipulate and hurt people without feeling guilty. They'll never try to see things from your perspective, because they're too focused on their own needs.

8. Envy: Narcissists are often envious of others, especially if someone else has something they feel they deserve. They constantly compare themselves to others and can become jealous if they feel overshadowed. In romantic relationships, this can lead to controlling or possessive behavior. If they see someone else getting the attention they crave, their jealousy can turn into rage.

9. Arrogance: Finally, narcissists often come across as arrogant and condescending. They believe they are better than others and have no problem letting everyone know it. They'll roll their eyes, scoff at suggestions, and dismiss anyone who doesn't agree with them. This arrogance can make them difficult to work with or be around, as they refuse to accept any criticism or feedback.

The "Friend" Who Takes and Never Gives

I once had a friend who never had anything nice to say about me. I would go out of my way to compliment her—her hair, her clothes, her work—yet she never thanked or complimented me back. I kept trying to make her feel good, hoping that one day she'd reciprocate, but it never happened. She took all the compliments I could give and gave nothing in return.

One night at a party, after she'd had a little too much to drink, she admitted that she had always been jealous of me. Her admission explained her behavior, but by then, the relationship had already deteriorated beyond repair. That's the thing about narcissistic people: They'll take everything and give nothing. If you're in a relationship like this—whether it's a friendship, romantic partnership, or even a professional relationship—it's important to ask yourself if it's really worth it. If you find yourself in one of these one-sided relationships, it's time to take a step back and stop investing in someone who doesn't invest in you.

SOCIAL MEDIA AND NARCISSISM

Social media has created an environment where narcissistic behavior can thrive. Platforms like Instagram, TikTok, and Facebook allow individuals to curate a perfect image of themselves, often exaggerating their achievements, attractiveness, and success to gain followers, likes, and validation. While most people who use social media aren't narcissists, it's a system that rewards narcissistic tendencies.

Consider the influencer who posts daily about their "perfect" life: luxurious vacations, expensive meals, flawless appearance. Behind the scenes, they might be struggling with the same insecurities and challenges as everyone else, but their online persona is carefully crafted to garner attention and admiration. Social media, lending itself so well to the manipulation of others' perceptions, is a breeding ground for narcissism.

Machiavellianism: The Manipulator's Quest for Power

If narcissism is about self-obsession, Machiavellianism is about power. The term comes from Niccolò Machiavelli, a 16th-century political philosopher who wrote *The Prince*, a book that advised rulers to use deceit, manipulation, and even cruelty to maintain power. In Machiavelli's view, the ends justified the means, no matter how unethical the actions taken to get there.

In modern psychology, Machiavellianism describes someone who will stop at nothing to get what they want. These individuals cunning and strategic, and have no problem deceiving others to achieve their goals. They're often charming and smooth talkers, using their wit to manipulate people without being detected. A person exhibiting Machiavellianism may not show the same need for admiration as a narcissist, but they are just as dangerous in their willingness to exploit others. They have a singular focus on gaining control, money, or influence, and they're willing to lie, cheat, or hurt others in their quest to get it.

Traits of Machiavellianism

1. Strong desire to control: The hallmark of a Machiavellian individual is their ability to manipulate others so they can have power and control over them. They excel at persuading others to do things that serve their own interests, often without the other person realizing they're being used. In personal relationships, this might look like someone who dominates the other person by controlling how much they spend, who they can be friends with, and which hobbies they're allowed. They want control over decisions that are meant to be personal and aren't theirs to make.

2. Lack of morality: Like narcissists, Machiavellians lack a strong moral compass. They don't see anything wrong with bending or breaking the rules to achieve their goals. In their minds, they can do anything they want to get what they desire.

3. Strategic thinking: Machiavellians are highly strategic and think several steps ahead. They plan out their actions carefully, always looking for the most effective way to get what they want. Whether in their business or personal life, they use people as pawns in their larger game.

REAL-LIFE PONZI SCHEMES AND MACHIAVELLIANISM

One of the most infamous examples of Machiavellianism in recent history is Bernie Madoff, who orchestrated one of the largest Ponzi schemes ever, defrauding thousands of people out of billions of dollars. Madoff built a reputation as a trusted financial advisor, using his charm and influence to convince people to invest with him. Meanwhile, he was using their money to fund his own lavish lifestyle, manipulating those who trusted him for his own gain.

Similarly, Barry Minkow, a teenage entrepreneur, built a multimillion-dollar business based on lies and deceit. Minkow started his company, ZZZZ Best, as a carpet-cleaning service, but quickly realized he could inflate the numbers to make it look like his business was far more successful than it really was. His company became a front for a massive Ponzi scheme, and by the time the fraud was uncovered, he had defrauded investors out of over $100 million. Even after serving time in prison, Minkow continued to commit financial crimes, showing how deeply ingrained Machiavellian traits can be.

4. Focus on power and money: While narcissists crave admiration and attention, Machiavellians are more interested in gaining status and wealth. They're often found in positions of authority, using their influence to control others and amass more resources.

5. Cynicism: Machiavellians tend to have a negative view of human nature. They believe that everyone is out for themselves, and they see relationships as transactional. This worldview makes it easy for them to justify their manipulative behavior—they assume everyone else is just as self-serving as they are.

Psychopathy: An Emotional Void

Psychopathy is the final piece of the Dark Triad, and it's often the most chilling. Many people associate psychopathy with violent criminals and serial killers, but the reality is that, though psychopaths have obsessive and extreme behavioral tendencies, they are not necessarily murderous. They're not always violent either, but they do lack empathy and remorse, and their unfeeling behavior makes them a threat to others.

Unlike narcissists and Machiavellians, psychopaths are often more calculated in their approach. They can be charming, charismatic, and appear completely normal on the surface. But underneath, they are cold, calculating, and completely detached from the emotions of others. Psychopaths are capable of lying, cheating, and manipulating without feeling any of the guilt or shame that would stop a typical person.

Traits of Psychopathy

1. Lack of empathy: Psychopaths are incapable of feeling empathy or remorse. This means they have no problem hurting others, whether emotionally or physically, because they can't look at their behavior from an outside perspective. They simply don't care about, or see anything wrong with, the pain they cause others. They lack the ability to gut-check their actions against a moral code because they have no moral code.

2. Superficial charm: One of the most dangerous aspects of this disorder is that psychopaths often come across as charming and charismatic, which makes it easy for them to gain the trust of others. But this charm is only skin-deep, and once they've gained someone's trust, they have no problem using or discarding them.

REAL-LIFE PSYCHOPATH: CHARISMA AND DECEPTION

One of the most infamous psychopaths in history is Ted Bundy, a serial killer who confessed to murdering thirty women in the 1970s. As a kid, he would buy mice at a local pet store, then "play God" with them by rounding them up in a corral and deciding which to kill or spare. This desire to exert control on other living beings foreshadowed the crimes to come. Bundy was known for his good looks, intelligence, and charm, which allowed him to lure his victims into trusting him so he could commit his brutal crimes. His tactics included playing the helpless, charming guy in need of assistance (he would keep fake casts, arm slings, and crutches in his car) or posing as a cop to gain credibility. Bundy's ability to appear normal, even likable, made him one of the most dangerous psychopaths in history. People simply couldn't believe that someone so charming could be capable of such horrific acts.

REAL-LIFE PSYCHOPATH: KILLER CLOWN CHARM

John Wayne Gacy was a seemingly successful businessman and beloved community member, even hosting political fundraisers and volunteering to perform as a clown at charity events and kids' parties. But behind that facade, he lured young men to his home, murdered them, and buried their bodies in the crawlspace of his house. Gacy's manipulative charm allowed him to hide his true nature from those around him for years, until the sheer scale of his crimes came to light. Like Bundy, Gacy had a troubled childhood marked by abuse and an inability to form healthy social relationships, a common thread among many with psychopathic tendencies.

3. Impulsivity: Psychopaths often act on impulse, driven by a need for excitement or a desire to dominate others. They don't think about the consequences of their actions, and they rarely feel any regret if they hurt someone along the way.

4. Manipulation: Like Machiavellians, psychopaths are skilled manipulators. They use charm, deceit, and intimidation to get what they want, whether it's money, power, or control over others. The difference is that psychopaths are more detached from the emotional fallout of their actions.

5. Lack of fear: Psychopaths don't experience fear in the same way that most people do. This makes them more willing to take risks and engage in reckless behavior. It also makes them harder to control or reason with, as they aren't motivated by the same regard for consequences that guide most people.

Psychopathic Killer Traits

Not all psychopaths are killers, but among those who are, these are the overlapping traits and warning signs:

- Abnormal, difficult childhoods with parental problems (physical, mental, emotional abuse and deceit)
- Socially awkward/antisocial behaviors as pre-teens and teenagers, with a tendency to be loners and act impulsively and aggressively toward humans and animals
- Trustworthy, appealing façade to cover their true nature
- Thirst for dominance, power, and control over others
- Obsession with sadism
- Lack of empathy, remorse, guilt, shame, morals, and ethics

The common traits of the Dark Triad—narcissism, Machiavellianism, and psychopathy—are coldness, a lack of empathy for others, and a willingness to use others for their own enjoyment or advancement. While not everyone who uses dark psychology will exhibit these traits to the extreme, it's important to recognize the signs so you can protect yourself from being manipulated or taken advantage of. If you find yourself in a relationship with someone who displays these traits, whether it's a romantic partner, friend, or coworker, the best thing you can do is set clear boundaries. Don't try to change them—they won't change, no matter how much you want them to. Instead, focus on protecting your own well-being and removing yourself from the situation if necessary.

As you continue reading, I'll guide you through strategies for dealing with individuals who exhibit dark psychological traits. From setting healthier limits to recognizing manipulation tactics, you'll learn to use persuasion tactics and other tools to protect yourself from the harm that these individuals can cause. Become an expert at managing the Dark Triad and you'll be better equipped to navigate the challenges that come with dealing with toxic people in your life.

2

PERSUASION VS. DARK PSYCHOLOGY

LET'S BE CRYSTAL CLEAR: There is no positive use for dark psychology, and this book does not promote it. Social media buzzes with advice, especially on platforms like TikTok, that encourages women to use dark psychology to "gain the upper hand" in relationships. But manipulation, in any form, is toxic. It's a strategy that may get you what you want in the short term, but it damages trust, undermines relationships, and ultimately harms both parties involved.

Dark psychology is built on taking advantage of others—financially, emotionally, mentally, and physically. It's a blueprint for manipulation, coercion, and deceit. Some examples of manipulation include:

- Forcing compliance through intimidation or pressure
- Laying down demands and expecting others to obey without question
- Cherry-picking data or information to support a position, while ignoring opposing facts

- Aggressively pushing for a resolution, leaving the other person no room to think or disagree

Now contrast that with persuasion, which is an entirely different act. Persuasion is a positive, ethical skill—one that can actually help you protect yourself from manipulators. Throughout my career, including my time as a military interrogator, I've relied on persuasion to get to the truth. Persuasion builds trust, while dark psychology destroys it.

THE PRINCIPLES OF PERSUASION

According to the psychologist Robert Cialdini, a leading author and expert in the field, persuasion rests on six key principles:

1. Reciprocity: People feel inclined to return a favor when someone does something kind for them.

2. Commitment and consistency: Humans like to stick to their values and commitments because it aligns with their self-image.

3. Social proof: We tend to follow the crowd; if others are doing something, we often assume it's the right choice.

4. Authority: We're more likely to trust and follow people who demonstrate expertise or have a strong reputation.

5. Liking: We're easily persuaded by people who are similar to us or whom we genuinely like.

6. Scarcity: When something seems rare or in high demand, it becomes more appealing.

These principles are used in everything from sales to negotiations, including conflict resolution, decision-making, and even securing investors. They offer a way to influence others while maintaining respect and integrity. For instance, in a sales pitch,

REAL-LIFE ENCOUNTERS: TERRORISM AND DARK PSYCHOLOGY

In my own life, I've had plenty of encounters with individuals who fit the profile of the Dark Triad, particularly during my time working as an interrogator at Guantanamo Bay after the 9/11 attacks. The detainees I questioned were deeply committed to their beliefs, which often included a radical interpretation of Islam that justified violence against others. These individuals were so entrenched in their ideology that they felt no regrets over what they had done and had no empathy for their victims. It was impossible to reason with them as to why their actions were wrong.

I quickly learned that trying to reason with someone driven by dark psychological forces was futile. They had been brainwashed and manipulated themselves. With no choice of free thought, they had to conform to beliefs that were instilled in them, even if those beliefs meant killing innocent people. Instead, I had to take a different approach—one that involved listening and using elicitation techniques to encourage them to open up to me. The more they opened up, the easier it was to outsmart them or get key information from them.

emphasizing how your product is running out (scarcity) or pointing out that others have already bought it (social proof) can be effective in persuading someone to make a purchase.

Power Yourself from Within

Despite what social media may tell you, dark psychology does not empower you. Manipulating others weakens you. True empowerment comes from increasing your emotional intelligence, building trust with others, and developing resilience. It's about being confident in your own abilities, learning from your mistakes, and nurturing an inner strength that no one can take away from you.

Emotional intelligence—your ability to navigate change, adapt, and learn from setbacks—is the real key to empowerment. It means being open to feedback, even when it stings. It's about having the courage to admit when you're wrong and still push forward. If you feel the need to manipulate others to feel better about yourself, it's time to pause and rethink your approach.

I understand the temptation to "fight fire with fire" in a toxic relationship, especially for women who feel they're not getting the respect they deserve. I faced similar challenges during my military career. But I earned respect—not by trying to mimic the behavior of men around me, not by using dark psychology, but by embracing my unique strengths. I didn't need to manipulate or pretend. My expertise, leadership skills, and confidence spoke for themselves. In fact, being a woman was an advantage in many situations. As a female interrogator, I could build rapport quickly. I wasn't seen as a threat, which helped detainees feel comfortable enough to talk. Respect was given to me because they could tell that I was credible and competent. The men I served with respected me because of my authenticity, and I reciprocated.

How to Use Persuasion for Good

If you want to persuade others ethically or use persuasion to protect yourself from someone who's trying to manipulate you, here are five tactics that can help you change someone's behavior for the better:

1. Use logic and facts: Back up your argument with undeniable data. People, whether they're deceptive or not, trust logic, especially when you present it in a way that is hard to refute.

2. Form a coalition: Create a sense of collaboration, not opposition. When people feel like they're part of the decision-making process, they're more likely to agree with you.

3. Appeal to inspiration and motivation: Understand what drives the person you're speaking to. Tailor your message to their personal values and aspirations.

4. Reciprocity: Offer something of value first. It could be a favor, kindness, or an incentive. People naturally want to

---

REAL-LIFE PERSUASION TACTIC

One of the most effective techniques I've used in my career as an interrogator is called Assign a Positive Trait. It's simple but powerful. Here's how it works: When someone lies to me, instead of confronting them about their lies, I compliment them on their honesty, and that persuades them to be more truthful. For example, I might say:

- "You're the kind of person who takes responsibility and stands by their actions."
- "I know your family respects you for always being honest."
- "You've got strong morals, and people admire you for that."

After I make a positive statement about a person, I remain silent and give them time to think. Nine times out of ten, the person will tell me the truth. Why? Because deep down, most people want to be (and be seen as) good, honest individuals— even if they're caught in a lie. This technique taps into their desire to be consistent and keep a positive self-image. When my interviewees told me the truth, they felt relieved and thanked me for allowing them to be honest—even the ones who knew that being honest would come with a price. That's the power of persuasion: It influences behavior without crossing ethical lines.

reciprocate when they feel they've been given something. They also want to meet people halfway when there is an absurd demand—think negotiation!

5. Leverage authority and alliances: Sometimes, you need to rely on your own expertise or bring in support from trusted colleagues to strengthen your position.

At the end of the day, healthy, functional relationships worth being a part of—whether in business or personal life—are built on trust and respect. Manipulation will always destroy that foundation, leaving both parties worse off. Persuasion, on the other hand, builds trust and strengthens relationships. It allows you to influence without compromising your integrity.

Don't be tempted to resort to the tricks and shortcuts of dark psychology. When you lead with honesty and kindness, others will naturally trust and follow you.

As my husband, a Marine, often says, "Never mistake kindness for weakness." You can be kind yet firm in your boundaries with others. You can be compassionate but also decisive about who you want to let into your inner circle and what you are willing to tolerate.

MOST LIKELY TO DECEIVE: PEOPLE AND PERSONALITY DISORDERS

IN CHAPTER 1, WE BROKE DOWN THE CONCEPT OF THE DARK TRIAD: narcissism, Machiavellianism, and psychopathy. The traits of the Dark Triad are often associated with manipulative behavior, but dark psychology extends beyond those three archetypes. There are several other personality profiles and disorders that can make individuals more prone to using deception, manipulation, and coercion.

Consider the core principles of psychology: Sigmund Freud described the human psyche as divided into three parts: the id, the ego, and the superego. The id is where our most primitive desires live—things like aggression, sexual impulses, and unchecked urges. The superego acts as our moral compass, constantly reminding us of right and wrong, while the ego plays the role of mediator, trying to balance these forces. For most of us, the superego wins the battle. But for those who engage in dark psychology, the id often takes the wheel. To them, it's all about the primitive desire for and the pursuit of power, money, and dominance, whatever the cost.

THE DRIVE FOR POWER AND CONTROL

What motivates someone to manipulate or harm others? The answer often lies in a deep hunger for control—control over money, people, and outcomes. For some, this need is so powerful that they will stop at nothing to satisfy it, even if it means committing crimes or emotionally devastating those around them. They may manipulate, lie, and gaslight others to achieve their goals.

PERSONALITY DISORDERS AND DARK PSYCHOLOGY

Several personality disorders can predispose people to using dark tactics. Individuals who fall into these categories often struggle to connect with others in meaningful ways, which can lead to toxic and manipulative behaviors. Some of the most common disorders tied to manipulative behavior include:

1. Antisocial Personality Disorder (ASPD): Often referred to as sociopaths, individuals with ASPD lack empathy and have little regard for the rights or feelings of others. They may act impulsively, lie, and break rules with no remorse for the harm they cause. Think of someone who's always looking for an angle to exploit, whether they're an internet troll discrediting you online or a sibling who manipulates you into covering for their destructive behavior.

2. Borderline Personality Disorder (BPD): People with BPD often experience intense emotions and instability in their relationships. They may act impulsively, leading to frequent arguments, breakups, and reconciliation cycles. If you've ever been in a relationship where every small disagreement spirals into a massive argument, so you're always walking on eggshells, you might have encountered someone with BPD.

3. Histrionic Personality Disorder (HPD): Individuals with HPD crave attention and tend to overdramatize situations to stay in the spotlight. They can be emotionally volatile, often using their charm to manipulate others into giving them what they want. Imagine working with someone who turns every office interaction into a theatrical performance, constantly drawing attention to themselves and spinning minor events into major dramas. That's HPD in action.

HOW PERSONALITY DISORDERS CAN MANIFEST IN RELATIONSHIPS

People with personality disorders don't come with warning signs. There is no one behavior that will give them away, but the following examples show how some of the personality disorders above can play out in everyday, toxic ways:

- **The self-serving colleague:** You might work with someone who consistently takes credit for group projects, manipulating the situation to make themselves look good to the boss. They disregard the hard work of others and push blame elsewhere if something goes wrong. This person could have antisocial personality disorder—being more than willing to step on others to get ahead, with no remorse for who they leave behind.

- **The easily triggered partner:** Imagine you're in a relationship where your partner flies off the handle for minor reasons. Small fights turn into huge ones where they unleash damaging insults followed by dramatic romantic gestures to make up for their behavior. If you've ever been in a roller-coaster relationship like this, where you're tip-toeing around your partner and doing things "their way" to avoid conflict, your partner might have had borderline personality disorder.

- **The overly emotional friend:** Let's say you have a friend who's always at the center of every crisis. Whenever they don't get their way, they threaten to cut off the relationship or dramatically declare that no one ever cares about them. This is classic histrionic behavior. They use emotional extremes to keep others around them on edge, ensuring they stay the center of attention.

So what can you do if you suspect you're dealing with these personality disorders that have dark psychological tendencies? The first thing to remember is that only a trained mental health professional can diagnose personality disorders. However, if you're noticing warning signs or troubling behaviors, such as gaslighting, victim-blaming, and emotional coercion, then you need to take a stand against them.

It's important to remember that while personality disorders can drive people to use dark psychology, not everyone with a personality disorder is dangerous. However, when manipulation becomes a pattern, it's a sign that something is off, and you need to take steps to protect your peace and well-being. The 13 Power Moves laid out in Chapter 8 will help you do this.

DON'T LET STEREOTYPES CLOUD YOUR JUDGMENT

Biases are assumptions with no evidence to back them up. They might come from parents, family and friends, what we see on social media, or our education and upbringing. For a clearer read on people, it's best to at least be aware of your inherent biases for or against them. That way, you can put aside and avoid trusting those biases too deeply. Here are six common types of biases that could cause you to misjudge someone as innocent when they're deceptive (or vice versa):

- **The stereotype bias:** This is when we expect a group or a person to have certain qualities without knowing them personally. Some stereotypes we typically buy into assign character traits to those of a certain gender. We judge people by their dialect, clothing, hygiene, job, body art, home town, car, age, education, and so on. We might even positively stereotype confident people as trustworthy, even though there's no truth to that. (Ted Bundy may have been a handsome, eloquent guy, but women who trusted him because of those qualities ended up dead.)

- **The "similar to me" bias:** This is when we perceive someone to be like us because we have something in common, so we automatically like or favor them without knowing much beyond this common trait. This bias can be a serious safety breech. We tend to find it easier to trust people who like the same things or are from the same geographical area. Such commonalities might give us a good rapport with someone, so we let our guard down. Some people purposely try to be like us so that we like them. It's key to remember that people who are similar to us can still be a danger to us.

- **The halo-effect bias:** This is when we rate individuals either too highly or too low based on a trait, an overall impression, their role, status, age, job, or popularity. We can easily be fooled. An excellent example of this is how fans of champion cyclist Lance Armstrong handled the accusations against him. No one wanted to believe that he took performance-enhancing drugs to win the Tour de France because he was handsome, confident, and, perhaps most powerful in our minds, a cancer survivor. How could a cancer survivor lie and cheat? That's the halo-effect bias. Armstrong even used this bias to further confuse us, making us think it was crazy not to believe him. In a 2013 documentary, we hear him say, "To think that I'm gonna come back into the sport [after cancer] and risk my life with performance-enhancing drugs is crazy." Why would Lance—who beat cancer—lie? Simple: to win the Tour de France.

Someone whose judgment is clouded by the halo effect might jump to a false conclusion and trust the wrong person. They might tell themselves, "She is one of the top-rated scientists on this project, so I should adapt to her high-handedness" or "He's in school to become a doctor, so there is no way he would mistreat his girlfriend like that."

- **The "if they're doing it" bias:** This is the probability of adopting a belief because others have adopted that belief. Just because someone trusts your manipulative friend or coworker doesn't mean that you should. Consider the NXIUM cult leader Keith Raniere, who is now in prison on charges of attempted sex trafficking, forced labor conspiracy, wire fraud conspiracy, and racketeering. Raniere gathered quite a following and successfully recruited women, even famous actresses, to join his inner circle, where they were branded and coerced to perform sexual favors on him. He was very persuasive and could get his followers to think and act how he wanted them to, even if it went against their own moral code. The women who joined were most likely influenced by the fact that other women, even women of some fame, had joined the inner circle.

- **The confirmation bias:** This is when we tend to listen only to information that confirms our preconceptions, and consequently, we disregard any information that may contradict our preexisting views. This bias can have a negative impact on an investigation and make it more difficult to detect deception. Sometimes interviewers cannot let go of a confirmation that a person is guilty or lying, even when deceptive analysis supports that they are truthful, and vice versa. If you have a preexisting view that

REAL-LIFE "TELLS": HOW TO SPOT A LIAR

Pro cyclist Lance Armstrong denied using performance-enhancing drugs in an interview featured in the documentary, *Cycling's Greatest Fraud: Lance Armstrong*. At the end of the interview, there was a tell: He shrugged his shoulders. This movement indicated his uncertainty about what he'd just said (which was, as we now know, a lie). The significantly elevated pitch of his voice also indicated anxiety about lying. A 2012 study of thirty-nine participants in a question-and-answer session found that when a subject was lying, their vocal pitch increased (Villar, Arciuli, and Paterson 2012, 123–32).

you're dating a good person, it may be more difficult and take longer to see the truth.

- **The bond bias:** This is when you feel like part of a group, bonded by likes or dislikes, personality traits, commonalities, or experiences. When we bond with a person or group of people, we tend to trust those in the group and fear or dislike others outside the group. I see the bond bias frequently in companies divided into like-minded teams. For example, engineers tend to bond together tightly because they all speak the same technical language and work on similar projects. If they're approached by someone from the marketing or the sales department, communication may suffer because that person is considered an outsider and, therefore, different or untrustworthy. The group may shut them out, be curt, or become easily frustrated with them due to lack of commonality. On the other end of the spectrum, we may trust someone who's in our family or a work partner because we identify ourselves as part of the same bonded group.

Many times, we make decisions about people based not on facts but on assumptions about whether to like, trust, or believe them. There are a few ways to overcome these preconceptions to ensure that you are not being played by someone.

TECHNIQUES TO OVERCOME BIASES

To overcome our biases, we must be aware of them the moment they arise so we can consciously validate or reject them. If your brain leaps to an assumption about someone based on what you've heard about them, continue the conversation and dig for information to either back up that assumption or discredit it. If you find yourself immediately starting to like someone because you share the same interests, be cautious and reserve your judgment until you get to know them more deeply. Here are four techniques you can use to foster a clearer understanding of people and their behaviors unclouded by biases.

1. Ground your thoughts: Our thoughts can create an awareness barrier when our attention and focus are inward, not outward. When you notice that you are automatically responding in an emotional manner to someone's unwanted behavior, almost like a trigger, stop and refocus, especially if your response is not productive. Try to look at the person and the situation differently and without bias. For example, if your controlling spouse complains about you spending money and your natural response is to get mad and become defensive, try a new tactic. Instead, ask them a question such as, "Why do you feel that way?" When you don't get defensive, they won't. When you can stay calm, they will remain calm. Stop the whirlwind of thoughts in your head, because if you are focused on your own emotional reaction and personal thoughts, you can't address the person and their behavior. Bring your attention to the present; focus on your breath and what you see, hear, smell, or feel. When you tap into your senses, your mind stops jumping ahead. Instead of firing back, hold them accountable for their action and ask them questions about it.

2. Don't take it personally: Sometimes, we take what people say to us personally, even if that was not their intention. Try to see what others say to you through an objective lens. Do not react to what they say. Instead, be deliberate in your actions so you can hold them responsible and discover the truth.

3. Avoid expectations: Do not expect people in your life to be honest with you, respect you, or change for you when they have wronged you. Investigate their poor or unwanted behavior instead. Ask them for clarification as to why they did or said something. Then, ask them if they are willing to hear your side and how you feel. If they are unwilling to listen to you empathetically, you may need to seek another course of action or remove them from your inner circle. If you have expectations that the person will be respectful of and honest with you, you may unknowingly seek out information that validates your expectations instead of the truth (confirmation bias).

4: Confront your inner critic: If your inner critic is putting a halo on someone in your life who is taking advantage of you, you won't see it unless your question that voice in your head. If your inner voice tells you, "You deserve to be criticized because they know better than you," take a step back. It's possible that the halo bias is tricking you into thinking that the person you're involved with is too educated or well loved to hurt you.

DECEITFUL GAMES
AND TOXIC LIES

ALL OF US LIE. It's a universal part of being human. From the lies we tell to make others feel good or to avoid awkwardness to the more significant lies we tell out of self-preservation, deceit sneaks into our daily lives more often than we might like to admit. Some lies are relatively harmless, while others can be destructive and manipulative, especially when used to control or deceive. Because of my work and my professional experience, I am a human lie detector. I know when my family members and my friends lie to me. Do I call them out all the time? No. If they are lying to spare my feelings, or to make me feel comfortable and happy, I let it go. We all do that.

When we consider and study the different types of lies (and dig into the psychological mechanisms that drive people to lie), we can see more clearly how deception plays out in toxic relationships. We'll also look at clues for deception and preview some ways you can protect yourself from being a victim.

THE FOUR TYPES OF LIES

Not all lies are created equal. Different kinds of lies serve different purposes, from saving face in an uncomfortable situation to full-blown coercion. Consider, for a moment, the most common types of lies:

1. False statements: The simplest and most recognizable form of lying is making a statement that is completely untrue. False statements are easy to detect once the facts come to light, but they can still do a lot of damage, especially if the lie is told convincingly enough to be believed over time. Imagine someone telling you they finished a task that was assigned to them. They say, "I emailed it to you yesterday; you must have missed it." In reality, they never did the work. This false statement may buy them time, but it leaves you scrambling when the boss calls you both into their office to clear up the confusion. By the time the truth surfaces, trust is already damaged.

2. Embellishment: Have you ever been told a story that got a little more dramatic each time it was told? Maybe the fish they caught in Key West started off at five feet; later it's described as seven feet long. Or the black diamond trail your friend skied on their vacation got a little more dangerous every time they talked about it. That's embellishment. While embellishment might seem harmless, it can still be problematic, especially in professional settings. Let's say that a manager—we'll call her Samantha—keeps telling her team that her experience in a former job was crucial in winning a major contract. She mentions her pivotal role so often that people begin to see her as a key player in that company's success. But in reality, Samantha was only a junior member of the team, and her contributions weren't as significant as she claims. If this lie isn't detected, Samantha might be given more responsibility than she deserves at the new job and threaten the success of the company.

3. Distortion: Lying by distortion is when someone takes a mostly true story and twists part of it to fit their narrative. This might involve leaving out a key fact or exaggerating certain elements to create a misleading impression. Distortion is particularly damaging because it's harder to detect than an outright lie. For example, let's say Nora gets into an argument with her friend Ella. Afterward, she tells their mutual friends about the argument, but she conveniently leaves out the part where she insulted Ella first, focusing only on Ella's angry words. By omitting her own role, Nora creates a distorted version of the truth that paints her as the victim and Ella as the aggressor.

4. Omission: Omission is arguably the sneakiest form of lying because it involves leaving out important information that would change the other person's understanding of a situation. Unlike false statements, where the truth is directly contradicted, omission hides the truth without ever explicitly lying. This makes it much harder to detect. Imagine you're buying a used car. The seller tells you the car is in great condition and has never had any major issues. What they don't mention is that the car was in a minor accident two years ago. This omission may lead you to believe the car is in better shape than it really is, resulting in problems for you later on.

WHY WE LIE: THE PSYCHOLOGY OF DECEPTION

The motive behind lying is important to consider when you're trying to determine whether someone is using dark psychology in your midst. Understanding why people lie can help you distinguish everyday fibbing from self-serving deception.

Lying to protect feelings

One of the most common reasons people lie is to avoid hurting someone else's feelings. Think about the last time you told a friend they looked great in an outfit, even though you didn't really like it. You probably didn't want to make them feel self-conscious or embarrassed. This type of lie, often called a "white lie," is usually well-intentioned. While these lies might seem harmless, they can still create issues if overused. For example, if you consistently tell a partner everything is fine when it's not, you may avoid conflict in the short term but risk building resentment over time.

Lying for self-preservation

Another reason people lie is to protect themselves. We lie to avoid consequences, whether that means covering up a mistake at work or hiding something we're ashamed of in a relationship. Self-preservation lies can range from small fibs to massive deceptions, depending on the stakes.

For example, let's say a man was caught by his girlfriend

PSYCHOLOGICAL THEORY: HOW TO SPOT A LIAR

Research by Ekman and Friesen in the late 1970s on microexpressions (nonconscious facial expressions that appear for only about 1/15 to 1/25 of a second) shows that people's faces often reveal subtle clues when they lie, particularly when they are lying to mask their true emotions. Most people can't read microexpressions the way that experts can. Being aware of changes in facial expressions, especially ones that seem to conflict with body language and tone, can sometimes help you spot a lie before it grows into something bigger.

texting an ex late at night. When confronted, he panics and lies, saying, "She's just going through a rough time, and I was trying to be supportive." In reality, he is thinking about rekindling a relationship with his ex, but he doesn't want to deal with the fallout of admitting that to his girlfriend. His lie is an attempt to protect himself from the immediate emotional consequences of the truth.

Lying out of habit

Some people can't help but lie. Compulsive liars are not overtly manipulative. For them, truth-telling is awkward and uncomfortable; lying feels right. Many compulsive liars develop the habit early in life, especially if they live in an environment where lying helps them to cope or survive. A personality disorder like bipolar disorder, or a neurodevelopmental disorder like ADHD, might foster this particular kind of lying. Deception, for people who lie compulsively, is a way to avoid confrontation. Catching them, though, can be fairly easy because their stories and details rarely add up, and they exhibit the usual deceptive tells. They are very aware that they are lying, and they are likely to admit to their lies when challenged.

Lying to get your way

Pathological liars deceive for personal gain, with little regard or respect for the rights and feelings of others. People with mental health disorders like APD and NPD are more likely to be pathological liars. These are supremely confident liars; they will look you straight in the eye as they spin all sorts of untruths. They exaggerate, change their story often, and do not value the truth. If confronted, they will be defensive, and if they're caught, they will persist in denying the truth.

Those who use dark psychology are often con artists and liars who deceive for a self-serving purpose. On the high side of the malicious intention scale are those who lie to seek revenge, make others feel bad, hurt people, or get away with criminal behavior. From the compulsive liars for whom lying is a way of life to the charming psychopaths who lie incessantly to get their way with no concern for others, the goal of lying might be:

- Money
- Power/authority
- Control over a group (dictatorship) or a person (what they say, think, act)
- Manipulation
- Coercion
- Affection
- Attention
- Dependency (they want/need people to depend on them)
- Love
- Self-aggrandizement
- Self-preservation
- Revenge

LYING AND MANIPULATION TOOLS

Deceit is a hallmark of dark psychology. The tools (or as some might call them, weapons) of dark psychology vary widely, but they tend to include one or more of the following:

Gaslighting

One of the most dangerous forms of manipulation, touched on in Chapter 3, is gaslighting, a tactic whereby one person convinces another to doubt their own memory or perception of reality. The term "gaslighting" comes from the 1938 play *Gas Light*, where a husband slowly convinces his wife that she's going crazy so he can steal from her. Gaslighting is often used in abusive relationships, where the manipulator slowly chips away at the victim's confidence and self-trust.

My friends Erica and James had been dating for a year when Erica began noticing that James would often deny things that she clearly remembered happening. If she brought up a conversation from the previous week, James would say, "That never happened. You must be imagining things." Over time, James escalated his gaslighting, making Erica question everything from her memory to her emotional reactions. If she got upset about something he did, James would say, "You're too sensitive" or "You're making a big deal out of nothing." Eventually, Erica felt like she couldn't trust her own mind and became completely dependent on James for validation of what was real. She eventually sought counseling, opened up about what was happening to her, and decided to leave the toxic relationship.

Gaslighting is a powerful form of emotional abuse because it doesn't just manipulate the victim's actions—it manipulates their sense of reality. Victims of gaslighting often feel trapped, confused, and anxious, unsure of what is real and what is a lie.

Why It Works

According to Robin Stern, Ph.D., author of *The Gaslight Effect*, gaslighting works because it is gradual. The manipulator starts with small lies and distortions, slowly increasing the level of deceit until the victim is so confused that they don't trust their own perception of reality anymore. In Stern's research, she found that gaslighting is particularly common in relationships where one partner is emotionally vulnerable, such as someone recovering from a breakup, dealing with low self-esteem, or going through a difficult time in their life.

Guilt-Tripping

Guilt is another powerful tool of manipulation, especially in family dynamics and long-term relationships. When someone uses guilt to control another person, they make the victim feel responsible for their happiness, well-being, and emotional state. Guilt-tripping often works because it taps into our natural desire to be kind and supportive to the people we love. But when guilt is used as a weapon, it can create an unhealthy dynamic where one person is constantly sacrificing their needs to keep

THE POWER OF SUGGESTION: FALSE CONFESSION

In investigative work, detectives must be very careful when providing evidence to a suspect or suggesting hypothetical but plausible reasons for a suspect's actions, because they could cause the suspect to start doubting their own memory of the events. This is called memory distrust syndrome, or MDS. Let's say a detective is questioning a rape suspect, and during the questioning, they suggest that the suspect may not remember they raped someone because they passed out after drinking too much. Then the detective shows the suspect pictures of him drinking and kissing the rape victim. Then they tell him witnesses saw him enter the room alone with the victim. This can cause the suspect to start to believe what the detective says based on the story and evidence provided. It might lead to his falsely confessing to raping the victim, only because it makes more sense than trying to back up why he believes he didn't. People falsely confess for a number of reasons, including harsh interrogation tactics, exhaustion, and bowing down to authority figures, but the main one is memory distrust syndrome.

the other person satisfied. Over time, this can lead to resentment, burnout, and emotional exhaustion.

Many people can probably relate to my friend Mark, who grew up with a mother who constantly guilt-tripped him into doing what she wanted. If Mark didn't visit her every weekend, she would say things like, "I guess you don't care about me anymore" and "I won't be around forever, and you'll regret not spending time with me when I'm gone." These comments made him feel terrible, and even though he had a busy job and a family of his own, Mark found himself rearranging his life to keep his mother happy. Building up boundaries and insisting on space can safeguard someone who's being guilt-tripped from an unhealthy power dynamic.

Why It Works

Psychologist Susan Forward explores this dynamic in her book *Toxic Parents*, in which she describes how guilt-tripping is often used by controlling parents to keep their children emotionally tied to them. According to Forward, parents who guilt-trip often have unresolved emotional issues of their own, and they use guilt as a way to maintain control over their adult children.

Playing the Victim

Another subtle weapon of dark psychology is playing the victim. This involves the manipulator positioning themselves as the helpless or wronged party in every situation, thereby eliciting sympathy and support from others. While it's normal to seek support during tough times, constant victim-playing is a form of emotional manipulation that keeps others feeling guilty, obligated, or responsible.

Why It Works

According to Karyl McBride, Ph.D., author of *Will I Ever Be Good Enough?*, people who frequently play the victim often do so to avoid taking responsibility for their own actions. By casting themselves as the wronged party, they shift the focus away from their behavior and make others feel guilty for not doing enough to help them.

The Friend Who Plays the Victim

You might have a friend or family member who always portrays themselves as the victim in every situation, skillfully manipulating others to gain attention, sympathy, or even financial support. This can be a highly effective tactic for gaining control in relationships while avoiding an overtly aggressive stance.

Let's consider the example of Martin and his best friend, Tom. Tom was always down on his luck. Whenever they met up, the conversation revolved around Tom's problems—his car had broken down, his job was awful, his girlfriend had left him. Martin, being a good friend, would often help, whether that meant lending Tom money, giving him a place to crash, or just listening for hours on end.

However, over time Martin realized that Tom never seemed to take responsibility for his own life. He would complain about work but never make an effort to improve his situation. When Martin suggested solutions—like looking for a new job or budgeting his money—Tom would always have an excuse as to why he couldn't get a decent-paying job.

Eventually, Martin realized that Tom was using his problems to keep Martin's attention and avoid responsibility. By positioning himself as the perpetual victim, Tom could manipulate Martin into constantly taking care of him, both emotionally and financially. This dynamic left Martin feeling drained and resentful as their friendship became one-sided.

Playing the victim traps the other person in a cycle of caretaking. It's important to recognize when a friend's problems are genuine versus when they are being used as a tool to keep you in a position of emotional servitude.

Reverse Psychology

Reverse psychology is a tactic where someone gets you to do what they want by suggesting the opposite. At its core, reverse psychology leverages the very human desire for independence and control. When someone feels that their autonomy is being threatened, they might do the exact opposite of what's being suggested in order to reclaim a sense of power. In this way, the manipulator gains control without appearing to push for it.

In the workplace, you might experience this as someone saying, "You're probably too busy to help me with this project." While it seems like they're being considerate of your time, they're actually nudging you to say, "Let me help." It's a way to control your actions without directly asking for anything.

A partner who uses reverse psychology might say, "You don't have to spend time with me if you don't want to." On the surface, this seems like a neutral statement, but it can provoke feelings of guilt and obligation. The underlying message is, "You should want to spend time with me," and the person on the receiving end might feel compelled to prove that they do care by spending more time with their partner.

In relationships, reverse psychology can create a power dynamic where one partner subtly controls the other's actions. The partner using reverse psychology never directly asks for what they want, but instead manipulates the other into doing it for them. This form of manipulation is particularly dangerous because it's hard to detect—after all, it doesn't look like the person is asking for anything at all.

Why It Works

Reverse psychology relies on the principle of reactance theory, which was first introduced by psychologist Jack Brehm in 1966. Reactance theory suggests that when people feel their freedom to choose is restricted, they experience an unpleasant emotional response (reactance), leading them to assert their freedom by doing the opposite of what they've been told. This psychological resistance is strongest in individuals who value their independence and decision-making abilities.

Victim Blaming

Victim blaming is a common and toxic form of manipulation where the person responsible for harm deflects blame onto the victim. In relationships, this tactic is used to avoid accountability for abusive, harmful, or inappropriate behavior. By shifting the blame, the manipulator not only escapes responsibility but also makes the victim question their own role in the situation, often leaving them feeling guilty, ashamed, or confused.

A victim blamer who causes harm insists that the victim is, in some way, responsible for the abuse they suffered. This might sound like, "If you hadn't provoked me, I wouldn't have gotten so angry," or "If you weren't so crazy, I wouldn't have broken up with you." The goal is to make the victim feel as though they deserve the mistreatment or that their actions somehow caused it.

In romantic relationships, victim blaming often appears in cases of emotional, verbal, or physical abuse. The abuser might say, "You made me hit you by pushing me too far" or "If you didn't nag so much, I wouldn't have yelled at you." These statements shift the focus away from the abuser's behavior and onto the victim's supposed faults. Over time, victims may start to believe that they are to blame for the mistreatment they experience, leading to feelings of self-doubt, low self-esteem, and even depression. This makes it harder for victims to leave abusive relationships.

Here are some phrases and questions you might hear from someone who uses victim blaming as a tool for dark psychology:

You should have known better.

I told you not to trust them.

You shouldn't have been out that late.

You should have walked away when you had the chance.

We told you to leave him, but you wouldn't.

Did you say anything that could have been taken the wrong way?

Why didn't you tell anyone?

Why didn't you report it sooner?

How much were you drinking?

Do you think you could have provoked them?

Why It Works

Victim blaming taps into some of our deepest fears about vulnerability and control. It's human nature to want to believe that the world is fair and that bad things happen for a reason. This belief is known as the just-world hypothesis, and it's a coping mechanism that helps us feel safe. However, it also makes people more prone to blaming victims—if something bad happens to someone, we assume they must have done something to deserve it, because that makes the world feel more predictable and controllable.

For the person being blamed, this can be devastating. Victims of manipulation often find themselves questioning their own actions, asking, "Was it really my fault?" or "Did I deserve that treatment?" The manipulator exploits this self-doubt, keeping the victim trapped in a cycle of guilt and shame.

REAL-LIFE PROFILES IN DARK PSYCHOLOGY: THE VICTIM-BLAMING HUSBAND

As the interrogation expert on the show *Couples Court with the Cutlers,* my job was to interview the litigant to determine whether the accused was lying or telling the truth. One litigant, David, was accused by his wife of cheating. From the moment I started the interview, David kept telling me how insecure and crazy his wife was. He said she was so crazy that she put GPS trackers on his phone and his car. To me, these were classic smokescreen and victim-blaming moves. He was trying to gaslight me into believing that his wife's jealousy and insecurity were the main issues, but I knew better.

I developed a rapport with him in the green room and got him laughing and joking. But I knew that he was lying and that I would call him out on the show. When I did call him out, he admitted to lying and confessed to being promiscuous. It turns out he wasn't cheating on her with one woman; it was multiple women, multiple times a week. David was using dark psychology for his own self-preservation.

Victim blaming can also isolate the victim from support systems. If the victim starts to believe that they are responsible for the abuse, they may feel too ashamed or guilty to reach out for help from friends, family, or professionals. This isolation makes it even harder to break free from the manipulative relationship.

Negging

Negging is a manipulative tactic often used in romantic relationships, particularly in the early stages of dating. It involves giving someone a backhanded compliment, something that seems like a compliment on the surface but is actually a subtle insult. The goal of negging is to undermine the other person's confidence, making them feel insecure and, as a result, more likely to seek approval and validation from the person who negged them.

Negging is a classic move used by pickup artists who want to lower a woman's self-esteem so that she becomes more receptive to romantic advances. For example, a man might say, "You look like you're in shape. I bet if you worked out more, you would look amazing" or "You're smart—probably smarter than you look." These statements are designed to throw the recipient off balance. Instead of feeling confident and empowered, they suddenly feel insecure and unsure of themselves.

Why It Works

The psychology behind negging is that people, when faced with an insult, often seek to correct the imbalance or overcome the insult. They may start seeking validation from the person who insulted them in order to regain their confidence. The manipulator has planted a seed of insecurity and positioned themselves as the person who can give or withhold approval, thereby gaining control.

Negging is particularly insidious because it often leaves the victim feeling confused. The comment was technically a compliment, so why do they feel insulted? This confusion creates a desire to gain the manipulator's approval in order to resolve the discomfort.

HOW TO OUTSMART A LIAR

Detecting deception can be challenging, especially when the person deceiving you is skilled at hiding the truth. However, there are certain behavioral cues and patterns that can help you recognize when someone might be lying. I'll get deeper into proven strategies for getting to the truth later in this book, but here are some clues that are indicators of deception:

1. Inconsistent stories: One of the most obvious signs of deception is inconsistency in someone's story. If you notice details changing over time or facts that don't add up, it's possible the person is lying. When people tell the truth, their recollection remains stable because it's based on real events. But liars have to remember what they said previously, and that can lead to slips or contradictions. If you ask them to repeat a story and the version changes or key details are omitted, that's a red flag.

2. Too much or too little information: Liars often provide either too much detail or too little. Some try to cover their tracks by overexplaining every aspect of a situation, thinking that adding extra information will make them seem more credible. They might go off on tangents or include unnecessary specifics. Others, however, might provide too little information, giving vague answers or dodging direct questions. They may avoid providing details that could be easily checked or verified. Watch out for either extreme—both can be signs of deceit.

3. Body-language discrepancies: When someone is truthful, their body language and their words are in sync. When someone is lying, their body language may not align with what they're saying. For example, they might shake their head "no" while saying "yes," or vice versa. Liars may also exhibit closed-off body language, like crossing their arms or turning away slightly, as if to protect themselves from being exposed. Fidgeting, touching the face, avoiding eye contact, and excessive blinking can also be signs that someone is uncomfortable and possibly being deceptive. (You will learn more about this in Chapter 9, where I discuss the most accurate indicator of deception.)

4. Changes in voice or speech patterns: A person's voice can change when they are lying. Their pitch may become higher due to the tension and stress of lying, and they might begin to speak faster or more slowly than usual. Pauses and hesitations—especially in places where there shouldn't be any—are another clue. If someone suddenly becomes vague or hesitant when asked a direct question, they may be buying time to come up with a plausible lie. Watch out for people stumbling over their words or suddenly using fillers like "um" and "you know" more often than usual.

5. Evasiveness: Liars often deflect or evade questions to avoid giving a direct answer. They might respond to your question with another question or shift the focus of the conversation entirely. This could include changing the subject, bringing up unrelated issues, or redirecting the conversation back to you in an attempt to throw you off track. If they're consistently steering the conversation away from a particular topic or giving you half-answers, this could be a sign that they are trying to hide something.

6. Overemphasizing honesty: People who are lying often overcompensate by insisting they are telling the truth. They may use phrases like "To be honest," "I swear," and "Believe me" more than usual, trying to convince you of their sincerity. The more someone tries to emphasize their honesty, the more likely it is they feel insecure about whether you believe them.

While no single behavior definitively proves someone is lying, these signs—especially when combined—can give you clues. Trust your instincts, observe the person's patterns of behavior, and look for the inconsistencies that signal deception.

EMOTIONAL RED FLAGS FOR MANIPULATION

The first step in protecting yourself from manipulation is awareness. It can be subtle, creeping into everyday conversations and interactions until you start doubting your own perceptions. Asking yourself the right questions can help you clarify whether someone is controlling your behavior or emotions in unhealthy ways. Here are five key questions to ask yourself to determine if you're being deceived:

1. Do I feel guilty or anxious after most interactions with this person? One of the strongest indicators of manipulation is the presence of guilt or anxiety after you interact with someone. Manipulators often use guilt as a tool to control others, making them feel responsible for their happiness, their problems, or their emotional state. You might find yourself constantly worrying that you're not doing enough for them or that you're at fault for their struggles. If you frequently feel anxious or walk on eggshells around this person, it's a red flag that they may be manipulating your emotions to get their way.

2. Do I question my own memories or perceptions when they disagree with me? If you find yourself doubting your memories or feelings after a disagreement, it could be because someone is trying to make you question your own experiences. For example, if they dismiss your concerns by saying, "You're overreacting" or "That never happened," they might be trying to manipulate your perception of events. Over time, this can erode your confidence in your ability to interpret situations accurately, leaving you dependent on them to define reality.

3. Am I always the one compromising or apologizing?
Healthy relationships involve give-and-take, but manipulators often ensure the scales are tipped in their favor. Ask yourself if you're always the one who ends up apologizing, even when you're not at fault. Do you feel pressured to compromise on things that matter to you—your values, boundaries, or priorities—just to keep the peace? If you're constantly bending to accommodate their needs while your own go unmet, you may be in a manipulative relationship where your partner or colleague is using guilt or pressure to control you Are you constantly bending to accommodate their needs while yours go unmet? If so, you may be in a manipulative relationship where your partner or colleague is using guilt or pressure to control you.

4. Do they withhold affection, attention, or approval to get me to comply? Manipulators frequently use withholding tactics to control others. They might give you the cold shoulder, stop communicating, or withdraw affection when you don't do what they want. This leaves you feeling desperate to regain their approval or attention. If you notice a pattern in which their mood or treatment of you drastically changes depending on whether you're meeting their expectations, they could be using withholding as a manipulation strategy to keep you compliant.

5. Do I feel like I'm being "managed" rather than supported? In healthy relationships, both parties feel supported and valued. Manipulative individuals, however, tend to "manage" their relationships, treating the other like a resource they can use rather than a partner they respect. If you feel like your thoughts, actions, or decisions are being steered in a direction that only benefits them rather than something mutually beneficial, it's a sign of manipulation. You might also feel that they only show interest in your life when it serves their agenda rather than being genuinely supportive.

If the answers to these questions raise concerns, it may be time to reassess the relationship and set clear boundaries to protect yourself.

WHEN TO LISTEN TO FEAR

According to an article in *NeuroImage* titled "Amygdala activation when one is the target of deceit: Did he lie to you or to someone else?" the brain is programmed to send you a warning sign when you hear a lie. It actually triggers a fear response when someone is attempting to deceive you. If you find your fear activated by a particular person or their actions, then you may be getting this red flag from your brain. It may be telling you not to trust that person.

There are times, however, when fear is your enemy. If you fear standing up for yourself, taking a stand against someone manipulative, or saying no, you can put yourself in danger or get stuck in a toxic relationship. Later in this book, I will teach you how to have difficult conversations without fear to ensure your communication is clear and effective. Make no mistake: There are very scary people out there who can cause us grave harm. We need to identify the threat (strange behavior), investigate it (research, questioning, and conversational techniques), and know when to call out a person's inappropriate behavior or run from it. What we can't do is let our fear stop us from investigating it.

5

LOVE AND DARK PSYCHOLOGY

IN THIS CHAPTER, I'LL SHARE A FEW REAL-WORLD STORIES OF PEOPLE WHO PLACED THEIR TRUST IN THE WRONG PERSON. From almost getting scammed to surviving abusive relationships and facing the aftermath, these examples highlight how dark psychology infiltrates our most intimate bonds. It's easy to believe that these extreme cases of manipulation only exist in rare cases, but it's more common than we think. Every day, people find themselves gamed by those they love or trust, whether it's a new partner, a long-term boyfriend or girlfriend, or a spouse.

While the workplace might offer fertile ground for Machiavellians, romantic relationships often become breeding grounds for narcissistic behavior. People with NPD can be highly seductive and attentive at the start of a relationship, making you feel like you've found someone who truly sees you. They shower you with compliments, affection, and attention. It's intoxicating, and it pulls you in fast.

However, once they've secured your affection, the dynamic changes. What was once mutual admiration becomes a one-sided relationship, where they demand constant praise and validation while offering little in return. Narcissists have a way of making their partners feel like nothing is ever enough. You might find yourself constantly trying to please them, only to be met with criticism or emotional manipulation.

WHY DO PEOPLE FALL IN LOVE WITH MANIPULATORS?

If individuals with dark psychological traits are so harmful, why do so many people fall into their traps? Whether it's a narcissist, Machiavellian, or psychopath, these individuals often possess a set of skills that make them hard to resist—at least at first.

1. Charm and confidence: People with dark psychological traits are often extremely charming. They know how to make you feel good about yourself, at least initially. Their confidence can be intoxicating, especially if you're feeling insecure or vulnerable. They'll make you believe that they're the solution to your problems or that they see something special in you that no one else does.

2. Love bombing: In romantic relationships, narcissists often use a tactic called love bombing, where they overwhelm their partner with affection, attention, and gifts early on. This creates a sense of emotional intensity and makes the other person feel like they've found their soulmate. By the time the love bombing fades and the narcissist's true behavior emerges, the victim is already emotionally invested and may find it hard to leave.

3. Flattery and manipulation: Manipulators are skilled at knowing how to use flattery and emotional games to get what they want. They might make you feel indispensable or needed, only to turn around and exploit your loyalty for their own benefit.

4. Seeming normal: Psychopaths, in particular, are often very good at appearing completely normal—even likable. They can hold down jobs, maintain relationships, and project an image of stability, all while hiding their true lack of empathy and self-serving motives. This makes it difficult for others to recognize their dangerous traits until they're already romantically involved.

Profiles in Dark Psychology: A Husband with a Hidden Dark Side

A close friend of mine named Molly endured a toxic marriage. By the time we met, she was already divorced, and I only knew her as a strong single mom running her own business and excelling as a weapons expert. Over time, as our friendship deepened, she opened up about her past and the terrifying abuse she survived.

Her ex-husband, a high-powered politician, seemed like the perfect partner at first—successful, intelligent, and well-respected. However, as their marriage progressed, his darker side began to surface. He manipulated her emotions, beat her, and controlled every aspect of her life. Yet, as is often the case with abusers, he managed to keep his true nature hidden from others, including their children. He was good at seeming normal. (She later shared how he secretly quit his job right before their court hearing, making it seem like he had no income. The result? Molly was forced to pay him child support despite the fact that he was her abuser.)

Living in constant fear of his unannounced visits, violent outbursts, and manipulative tactics, she built a panic room in her home. Her health deteriorated from the stress, and no doctor could identify the cause. It wasn't until she worked with a therapist that she realized her physical ailments were a direct result of years of emotional abuse.

Her story is a powerful reminder that abuse isn't always visible to others. Emotional abuse, gaslighting, and manipulation can leave scars that take years to heal. Fortunately, Molly eventually found the strength to break free, and today she is in a loving and healthy relationship. Still, the fear and trauma she experienced serve as a warning to others about the depth of the damage dark psychology can cause.

True-Crime Profile in Dark Psychology: Drew Peterson

Drew Peterson was a police officer who worked for the police department in Bolingbrook, Illinois, a suburb of Chicago, for thirty years beginning in 1977. He retired in 2007 at the age of fifty-three and is currently serving a thirty-eight-year sentence in prison for murdering his third wife. Peterson had been married four times. His first wife, Carol, married Peterson in 1974 but divorced him six years later after finding out he was cheating on her. He married Vicki, his second wife, in 1982. During Vicki's ten years of marriage to Peterson, she accused Peterson of domestic violence. She divorced him after she found out he was cheating on her with a woman named Kathleen, who would become his third wife.

Peterson married Kathleen in 1992, just months after divorcing Vicki. His marriage to Kathleen ended in divorce on October 10, 2003. Not only was he cheating on Kathleen with his soon-to-be fourth wife, but during the final year of this marriage, the police were called to Kathleen's house numerous times for domestic violence. Kathleen and Drew Peterson shared custody of their two sons.

On October 18, 2003, just eight days after his divorce from Kathleen was finalized, Peterson married his fourth wife, nineteen-year-old Stacy (Peterson was forty-nine years old at the time). Peterson and Stacy lived less than a mile from Kathleen and their two sons. Stacy and Peterson also had two children of their own, a boy and a girl. On March 1, 2004, just a few months after Peterson and Stacy married, Kathleen's body was found naked in a dry bathtub in the house she and Peterson had lived in as a married couple. Kathleen's death at the time was ruled as accidental drowning.

On October 29, 2007, Stacy's sister reported her missing. Drew Peterson went on numerous TV news stations and told the world he believed she ran off with another guy. It was reported in several news outlets in November of 2007, including the *Chicago Sun Times* and CBS news, that Stacy told her pastor she was afraid of her husband. Stacy said that Peterson told her that he killed Kathleen and made it look like an accident. She said her husband had coached her on how to lie to police.

During the investigation into Stacy's disappearance, Drew Peterson often appeared arrogant and cocky to those investigating him. He sometimes wore the "Duper's Delight" grin, a term coined by psychologist Dr. Paul Ekman. Also described as the "cat who ate the canary" grin, this unwitting smile appears when a liar feels they successfully got away with a lie. At one point, in the midst of doing multiple TV appearances after Stacy went missing, Peterson suggested there should be a "win a date with Drew Peterson" contest.

With suspicion mounting, police exhumed Kathleen's body to conduct further research. They were skeptical that she had died of accidental drowning. Dr. Michael Baden, a former New York medical examiner and expert on the HBO series *Autopsy*, conducted an examination on Kathleen's remains. He concluded that she had died of drowning, but only after a struggle. Her body had been placed in the tub. Her death was determined to be a homicide. On September 6, 2012, after a lengthy trial, Peterson was convicted of murdering Kathleen and sentenced to thirty-eight years in prison.

Let's consider the telltale signs of dark psychology in Drew Peterson:

- **Inflated sense of self-importance:** In a 2008 interview with Larry King, one that I use to teach about deceptive tells, Peterson says that he is not like "common people," people who work for phone companies and electric companies. He put himself in a higher social status because he was a cop. (In Chapter 9, when I discuss statement analysis, I'll share Peterson's exact quote and you'll see that it reeks of narcissism and psychopathy.)

- **Lack of empathy and remorse:** Drew Peterson's joke about starting a dating game during Stacy's disappearance, and his jovial behavior during interviews, indicate a lack of remorse.

- **Exploiting others for his own benefit:** Once he was done with a woman or a marriage, he would quickly move on to the next (or kill her). He cheated on his first three wives and left them for the next one. Two of his ex-wives claimed mental and physical abuse, and one says he threatened her life (saying he knew how to make it look like an accident). His fourth wife's body still hasn't been found.

Real-Life Profile: The Gaslighting Boyfriend

One of the most common forms of deception in relationships is gaslighting, when a person manipulates someone into doubting their perceptions, memories, or sanity.

A woman who used the pseudonym Nicole to share her story

described a troubling romantic relationship with her charming coworker in which she was confined by his strict and suffocating rules. He'd become angry and emotional over small things, like the simple act of wanting to carry her own passport, the mention of an ex, or the "rudeness" of opening her purse at dinner in front of his friends. He'd tell her he could do much better than her, then later when she'd dare to leave him, he'd curl up in a ball and cry. He convinced her at times that she was a cruel partner and an embarrassing idiot. She was exhausted from the emotional roller coaster she was stuck on, but he could be so loving and warm at times: "I adored him, and this incredible man had chosen me. He was troubled, and I had to help him. I knew I hurt him, so I wanted to make it better."

Her family adored him, and she was getting to the age when her biological clock was ticking. Everyone told her to hang on tight—that he was a catch. Eventually, the control issues became more extreme, so extreme that it became clear to her that she was being gaslighted. She wasn't allowed to fall asleep before him or to get any space from him. Because he was so all-consuming, she'd escape to the bathroom for hours with a book to be left alone. The final straw came when he took the bathroom hinges off because he couldn't bear to be separated from her. She knew she would never be able to satisfy his narcissistic needs, so she left with the support of her sister and eventually, in therapy, realized the extent of the psychological games he'd played.

Real-Life Profile: The Crafty Cheater

Interestingly enough, years earlier, Nicole's gaslighting boyfriend and coworker had tormented another woman named Elizabeth. Nicole and Elizabeth eventually met and found their shared experiences incredibly healing. Elizabeth had met Mr. Charming at work as well. His game with her was to tell her about an event, switch the date or time to when she was busy, and then blame her for missing the event. If it were dinner or a ball, he'd tell her he was forced to bring another date to it (so as not to look pathetic to other people) because of her mistake. She didn't feel like she had a leg to stand on if she objected to him bringing another woman. She'd been made to feel so stupid for "mixing up" the time or date that she let herself be convinced that his "innocent" platonic dates were just that. But of course they weren't. He'd cheated on her numerous times by this point. The only reason she discovered his affairs was because she'd acquired an STD from his infidelity.

When he seduced her roommate, she still didn't leave him, though she did get a prescription for Prozac to dull the pain. His affairs made her cling to him in the belief that everyone wanted what she had. She would try to hang onto him, though it was making her crazy. When she spotted him in a car in front of his house with another woman, the truth was too much to bear. She ended things, but the lies and the betrayal haunted her for years.

LOVE AND DECEPTION IN THE DIGITAL AGE

In today's world, scammers prey on vulnerable individuals who are seeking companionship and love, using dark psychology and lies to exploit their targets financially. Online scams are becoming increasingly sophisticated, using dark psychology to manipulate victims into giving up personal information or money. Scammers build trust by creating a persona that appeals to their victim's emotional needs—loneliness, a desire for connection, or even shared interests. By the time the scammer asks for money, the victim is already emotionally invested and more likely to comply. A close friend of mine, Kay, nearly became one such victim.

Kay, newly divorced, had just started exploring online dating. She was thrilled by the possibilities—so many profiles, so many potential matches. However, she met someone who seemed too good to be true. The man claimed to be an oil-rig worker, explaining that his work made maintaining regular communication, especially via phone calls or video chats, difficult. Kay was initially skeptical, but she let her guard down after weeks of text messaging.

He began with a small request, asking her for a new phone after allegedly dropping his into the ocean. He claimed that he was using a friend's phone to access the dating app. Fortunately, she reached out to me before sending one to him. I recognized the scam immediately and helped her spot the red flags: inconsistent stories, refusal to provide personal details, excuses to stay off video, and vague responses to specific questions about his job. Armed with this information, Kay confronted him, and he disappeared, along with his online profile.

Another case of online scamming involved a widowed woman who developed a close emotional bond with someone who claimed to be a doctor working abroad. They exchanged messages over the course of a few months before the scammer asked her for money to buy a plane ticket to meet her in New York City. She wired him the money, only to receive a message from him saying he'd been arrested upon entry to the United States and needed bail money. She sent him bail money. On the day they were supposed to finally meet in person, the man never showed. It was then that she realized she had been scammed out of $10,000. Her devastation wasn't just about the money—it was the betrayal. She had trusted him, shared her life with him, and allowed herself to believe in the possibility of love again. Her vulnerability was used against her. To make matters worse, her family ridiculed her for being so foolish.

Romance scams like this one are not uncommon. According to the Federal Trade Commission, romance scams cost U.S. victims $304 million in 2020 alone, with the average victim losing around $9,000. These scams typically follow a predictable pattern: A person establishes an emotional connection with their target, often through an online dating platform, before inventing a reason why they need money—whether it's for travel, medical expenses, or an emergency. Those who are trusting enough to send money have to deal with the resulting emotional and financial fallout.

TAKING AN HONEST LOOK AT YOUR RELATIONSHIP

Manipulation in relationships can be subtle, gradual, and difficult to identify, especially when you care deeply for the person involved. When you're falling for someone or in a long-term relationship where you've already invested years of your life in another person, it's easy to overlook the signs of a toxic partner and rationalize problematic behavior. It requires strength and courage to take an objective look at the person you're with, but it's essential that you do—especially if warning bells are ringing. Staying in a manipulative relationship will erode your sense of self-worth and make you doubt your instincts, and could ultimately ruin your life or threaten your well-being.

My husband says that when you start dating someone, you meet their representative, since most people begin a relationship as their best public-facing self. They dress impeccably, mind what they say, listen attentively, express interest and empathy, and display manners. When the honeymoon phase ends, you start seeing their true traits and behaviors. When I first met my husband, he wasn't as sarcastic as he is now. I was certainly not as impatient as I am now. Those kinds of surprises are normal and easily overlooked when the love and respect remain. The real problems occur when you marry someone whose representative is disguising their true nature and their dangerous, devious, and controlling behaviors.

I know plenty of women who have endured relationships with men who were manipulative, controlling, liars, alcoholics, and physically abusive. The perpetrators certainly didn't show that dark side at the beginning of the relationship. Instead they played their own best representative to disguise their true nature.

THE DECEPTIVE PARTNER PLAYBOOK

One way to gain clarity when you think you may be a victim of dark psychology is to ask yourself specific questions and look for patterns of behavior that are manipulative. The right questions will encourage you to reflect on your partner's actions *and* your emotional responses to those actions. Below are key behaviors to look for if you suspect that your partner might be manipulating you.

- **They push for commitment:** If the person you are dating seems anxious to label your relationship and is pushing you to commit to them, that could be an early warning sign that they want to control you. Take the time to decide on your terms when you want to commit. Being too hasty in this decision could expose you and your inner circle to the damage dark psychology causes. Committing to another person, whether that be dating them exclusively or marriage, means you are giving a person access to your home, your family, your friends, and, in some cases, your money and possessions. You need to really trust someone before you make that kind of leap.

- **They blame you for everything and play the victim:** For example, when a disagreement happens and you try to talk to them about being respectful, non-accusatory, and calm, they state that you just want to fight when clearly you are not trying to. If you can't talk openly with your partner, that's cause for concern. You shouldn't have to walk on eggshells around a romantic partner or fear giving them constructive feedback.

- **It's their way or the highway:** If your relationship rules aren't observed, but theirs are, you might have a serious problem. For example, if you need time to calm down after a fight, but they want to continue arguing, they need to step back. They can't ask for space and time to calm down if they don't offer you that same respect. Dating or being married to a hypocrite is a concern when you sense that they may want to have more control and power in the relationship.

- **They sabotage your confidence:** There are many ways that dark psychology erodes a person's belief in themselves. If you're enduring persistent ridicule, criticism, biting sarcasm, or backhanded compliments (negging), it's a sign that your partner might be using dark psychology to weaken your resolve.

- **They're extra jealous:** If your partner is jealous of your friends, coworkers, and family members, they may have problems with self-esteem and blame you for their feelings of inadequacy.

- **You engage in self-destructive behaviors to cope:** If you have grown weak against their controlling behaviors, deceit, and manipulation, if you have engaged in self-destructive behaviors such as drinking more than usual, taking drugs (prescription or not), neglecting your own health, or avoiding social gatherings, or if you stop enjoying simple pleasures like getting your nails done or going for a walk in the woods, these are all self-destructive behaviors. You are sacrificing your health and well-being for someone who is causing you pain. They don't deserve your self-sacrifice.

- **They exhibit passive-aggressive behavior:** If your partner is consistently exhibiting passive-aggressive behavior (indirect versus open and honest displays of anger or annoyance) and they will not take constructive feedback or stop, then it may be time to move on. Even if you notice them behaving this way to their friends and family early on, assume it won't change and that you won't always be spared the same treatment.

THE DEFINING QUALITIES OF A TOXIC RELATIONSHIP

Every relationship has its challenges to bear as well as its highs and lows. We put up with quirks in our partners and in our marriages because, in the scheme of things, we're happy with this person. But sometimes, we lie to ourselves about how bad things have become. Sometimes when we get a gut feeling that our relationship isn't quite right, our conscious brain, the prefrontal cortex, doesn't know what to do with the information. These checklists can help us verify our gut instinct with data and objective truths.

If you're wrestling with a gut feeling that something's deeply wrong in your relationship and you recognize any of the qualities below in your own relationship, it might be time to move on.

- Your relationship has sex but no intimacy (emotional closeness, friendship, love).

- There is an imbalance in the relationship. While you are constantly trying to please them, they tend to criticize you.

- They are selfish, and your wants, needs, and desires are no longer a priority to them.

- They start spending more time away from you than with you.

- There are more bad times than good times. They are negative, angry, and combative over small things.

- They never support your wins or success. They're more likely to get jealous and belittle you. Your partner should be your biggest fan, not your biggest critic.

- You often have to make excuses to family and friends for your partner's unacceptable behavior.

- You catch them in malicious lies they tell to hide financial, emotional, and sexual infidelity.

Consult the list above, but also ask yourself these basic questions: Are you truly happy with your partner? Do you love your partner unconditionally? Do you feel safe with your partner? Do you value your partner? You may want to end that relationship if the answer to any of those questions is no.

TURNING PAIN INTO POWER

The stories and scenarios shared in this chapter highlight the devastating effects of dark psychology in romantic relationships. But there's one common thread running through them: resilience. Whether by escaping an abusive marriage, avoiding an online scam, or recovering from the psychological damage of negging and victim blaming, most of these individuals eventually found the strength to break free.

Once you understand the tactics used by romantic partners—whether that's gaslighting, negging, victim blaming, or other forms of deceit—you can start to recognize the warning signs in your own relationships. By learning to trust your instincts, pulling back and demanding a healthy amount of space, and seeking support when needed, you can protect yourself.

Later in this book, we'll dive deeper into the 13 Power Moves you can use to defend yourself from emotional manipulation. You'll learn how to analyze statements, uncover hidden truths, and regain control of your interactions. Dark psychology can be poisonous, but knowledge is the antidote.

FAMILY AND DARK PSYCHOLOGY

WHEN DARK PSYCHOLOGY AND MANIPULATION SHOW UP IN FAMILY DYNAMICS, it can be uniquely challenging. Unlike friends, colleagues, or romantic partners, you don't get to choose your family. This lack of choice can make navigating manipulative or toxic behavior within your family feel incredibly difficult. The big question becomes: *How do you cope with someone who is supposed to love you unconditionally but constantly undermines you?*

Family relationships are fundamental. They shape how we view ourselves and the world. Yet, just like any other relationship, family ties can be fraught with control, and even abuse. Dark psychology can show up in your core relationships with parents, siblings, children, and extended family members.

ACTS OF DARK PSYCHOLOGY IN FAMILIES

While we've already covered the general signs of manipulation in relationships, there are some that are particularly prevalent in families. Family relationships often come with an extra layer of obligation and loyalty, which can make it even more difficult to recognize toxic behavior. Here are some signs that dark psychology might be at play in your family:

1. **Constant guilt-tripping:** Family members might use guilt to control your behavior. A parent may say, "After all I've done for you, the least you could do is ..." or a grown sibling might manipulate you by saying, "I guess you don't care about family if you can't even show up for dinner." Guilt is a powerful emotional tool that keeps you feeling indebted and obligated, even when you're being treated unfairly.

2. **Emotional blackmail:** Emotional blackmail is using threats to manipulate someone into doing what the person in a power position wants. In families, this might look like a parent threatening to cut you out of the will or withholding affection unless you comply with their demands. This keeps you in a constant state of fear that you'll lose love, money, or acceptance.

3. **Verbal or emotional abuse disguised as "tough love":** Sometimes verbal abuse is presented as a way to strengthen a child or sibling. A parent might say, "I'm only saying this because I care about you," right before delivering a blow that destroys your confidence. Backhanded comments from family that are framed as concerns can erode your self-esteem over time.

4. **The silent treatment:** Another classic form of manipulation within families is the silent treatment. It's a passive-aggressive way to control the situation by refusing to communicate. This tactic is especially powerful in families because it creates an environment where the person on the receiving end

feels anxious and desperate to resolve the issue, even when they've done nothing wrong.

If a family member stops talking to you for days or weeks without explaining why, and then expects you to fix the relationship, they're using the silent treatment to manipulate you. They want you to feel uncomfortable and responsible for repairing the relationship, even when they are at fault.

5. Playing the victim: Manipulative family members often cast themselves as the victim in every situation. No matter what the actual circumstances are, they manage to twist the narrative so that they appear wronged. For example, if you confront them about something they did, a sibling might turn the conversation around to say, "I can't believe you're accusing me of that when I've always been there for you." This tactic is particularly effective because it makes you question your own feelings and actions. You start to feel like the problem, even when you were the one who was hurt.

SYMPTOMS OF DARK PSYCHOLOGY IN FAMILIES

When the above tools of dark psychology are being put into play, families tend to have some or all of the following qualities:

- **Pervasive arguing:** Constant arguing over petty stuff and very little calm conversation.

- **Anxiety-spiked gatherings:** Maybe your sister is too aggressive and you fear her bombastic behavior in public; perhaps you know your brother-in-law is engaging in adulterous behaviors and you have to pretend you don't know; or your uncle tends to get drunk and say things that are inappropriate and then blames his poor judgment on the alcohol. Either way, you dread getting together with family.

- **Unpredictable and untrustworthy behavior:** One minute they might be friendly and fun-loving; the next they are screaming at you and name-calling.

- **Lack of respect for your beliefs and feelings:** For example, if you tell your dad that his biting sarcasm is hurtful, he may tell you to toughen up, that you are taking his sarcasm too personally.

- **Cruel behavior and lies:** They might sabotage your chances of success, fake illnesses so they can't help you, or lie to make themselves appear better.

- **Lack of respect for boundaries:** They visit anytime they want, they invade your privacy and space, they lack respect for your home and things, and they share your personal and private details with others.

REDEFINING WHAT'S NORMAL

Family dynamics can shape behavior in ways that often go unnoticed. From a young age, we learn how to interact with the world through our families, which makes it easier for manipulation to take root. When you've been conditioned to accept certain behaviors, it becomes your "normal." This is why it can take years to realize that a family member has been manipulating you all along.

Children who grow up in households where manipulation, control, or abuse is common may not even recognize these behaviors as abnormal. They might internalize guilt or fear as natural parts of love. A mother who constantly guilt-trips her child, for example, is teaching that child to equate love with obligation. This kind of conditioning is incredibly powerful. It can make you feel responsible for your family's happiness, well-being, or emotional stability. The thought of setting boundaries or pushing back against manipulative behaviors may feel impossible because it feels like you're betraying the family.

THE PSYCHOLOGICAL IMPACT OF FAMILY MANIPULATION

The emotional toll of family manipulation is profound. When your trust is betrayed by someone who is supposed to love you unconditionally, it can shake your entire sense of self. Here are a few common psychological effects of being manipulated by family members:

1. Low self-esteem: Constant criticism, guilt trips, or emotional blackmail can chip away at your confidence over time. You start to doubt yourself, and you may feel like nothing you do is ever good enough. This low self-esteem often extends into other areas of your life, affecting your relationships, work, and overall well-being.

2. Anxiety: Being around manipulative family members can lead to a constant state of anxiety. You might feel like you're always walking on eggshells, afraid of setting off an emotional landmine. This chronic stress can cause both physical and emotional exhaustion.

3. Difficulty setting boundaries: When manipulation is a regular part of your family dynamic, it becomes difficult to set boundaries because you're so used to accommodating others. You may find yourself unable to say "no" even when you want to, or you may struggle with guilt after asserting your needs.

4. Codependency: In families where manipulation and control are present, codependency can develop. You may feel overly responsible for a family member's emotions and well-being, to the point where you neglect your own needs.

To illustrate how manipulation can manifest in family relationships, here are some other common, real-world scenarios to consider.

The Sibling Who Plays the Victim

In some families, there's a helpless sibling whom you can never do right by. They blame everyone else when life doesn't go their way—especially you. If they can't find a job, they blame you for not helping them network. If their relationship ends, they say it's because you didn't offer enough emotional support. You end up feeling responsible for their happiness, even though you know it's not your fault.

The Narcissistic Parent

In another family, a parent may need to be the center of attention. If you achieve something, they downplay it or find a way to make it about themselves. If you try to talk about your problems, they quickly redirect the conversation to their issues. You grow up feeling like your needs and feelings don't matter.

The Guilt-Wielding Parent

In toxic families, some members may use guilt to control others, forcing them to behave in ways that benefit the manipulator. Consider my friend Sarah, whose mother, Helen, would often use guilt to get her way. When Sarah got her first job and moved out of the family home, Helen would constantly call, saying things like, "I'm getting older, and I don't know how long I have left. You never visit." If Sarah didn't immediately agree to visit, Helen would sulk, then call her and say, "It's so lonely here now. I don't cook dinner anymore, because what's the sense of cooking for one?"

The guilt weighed heavily on Sarah, and she found herself driving hours every weekend to visit her mother, sacrificing time for her own life and relationships. Helen's guilt-tripping didn't stop there. When Sarah started dating someone new, her mother would constantly make comments like, "It's nice you found someone.

I wish I could have companionship like that." Sarah felt torn between her own happiness and her mother's emotional needs.

This kind of guilt manipulation is deeply toxic because it exploits the natural love and responsibility children often feel toward their parents. The manipulator uses guilt to control the other person's behavior, ensuring that their needs are always prioritized at the expense of the victim's autonomy. Over time, this can divide a family and erode the bond between mother and child. Sarah eventually realized that her mother's behavior was unhealthy and worked with a therapist to set boundaries, learning that it was OK to prioritize her own life without guilt.

In some cases, the child is the manipulator. Consider the example of a middle-aged man who is still struggling to make smart life choices. He can't hold a steady job, parties too much,

DARK PSYCHOLOGY DEFENSIVE: BUILDING BOUNDARIES

Broken families require strong boundaries. This might be the hardest step, but it's essential. Clearly define what behaviors you will and won't tolerate. If your family member is manipulating you, set a firm and specific limit to show them that you are in control. Stick to it, even if they try to guilt you into changing your mind. In some cases, the boundary you choose to set is to limit contact with the family member.

This doesn't mean you have to cut them off entirely (unless that's what's necessary for your well-being), but reducing the amount of time you spend with them can lessen their influence on you. Putting up some walls doesn't mean you love your family any less—it means you love and respect yourself enough to protect your emotional and mental health.

and frequently asks his mom—who is well-off—for help with his rent. When she refuses to keep giving him money, he might say something to make her feel guilty like, "Mom, how can you let me suffer? I'm your only child! I'm trying to do the right thing. I can't believe you won't help your son."

Family manipulation can be one of the most difficult forms of manipulation to address because of the deep emotional ties involved. But just because someone is family doesn't mean they have the right to control, manipulate, or abuse you. You have the right to protect yourself, set boundaries, and choose how much access someone has to your life.

Remember, the most important relationship you have is the one with yourself. You deserve to be treated with love, respect, and care—especially by family. If a family member isn't capable of that, it's up to you to protect your well-being and decide what role, if any, they will play in your life moving forward. By recognizing manipulation for what it is, you can take back control and eventually learn to step into your power.

THE WORKPLACE AND DARK PSYCHOLOGY

THE WORKPLACE IS OFTEN WHERE WE SPEND THE MAJORITY OF OUR WAKING HOURS, and it's supposed to be a place of collaboration, growth, and respect. But when dark psychology enters the equation, it can make going to work feel like walking onto a battlefield. Professional relationships are often plagued by the same problems and complexities we face in our personal relationships, but the stakes are very different. Your livelihood, your reputation, and even your mental well-being can be affected by the toxic behavior of coworkers, bosses, and those who report to you. When dark psychology sneaks into the office, it can disrupt your professional growth and your peace of mind.

The key is to recognize manipulative behaviors early and take steps to protect yourself. Whether you're dealing with a deceitful colleague or a self-serving boss, you can regain control of your work environment by trusting your instincts and documenting everything. You can develop and sharpen your instincts so that you recognize dark psychology tactics and deception before it goes too far.

PSYCHOPATHY IN LEADERSHIP ROLES

Despite sometimes being portrayed as violent criminals, many psychopaths hold high-status positions in society, particularly in leadership roles. Their charm, intelligence, and fearlessness can help them climb the ranks in business, politics, and other fields. However, because they lack empathy, their leadership style is often ruthless, self-serving, and damaging to those who work under them. Consider a CEO who makes reckless decisions that hurt employees, all for the sake of maximizing profits. They might lay off half the staff, cut corners on safety, or even engage in illegal activities—all while maintaining a calm demeanor and using their charisma to avoid detection. Employees might first be drawn to their confidence and decisiveness, but over time, they realize that the CEO's actions are driven by personal gain rather than the well-being of the company or its people.

A REAL-LIFE PSYCHOPATH AT WORK: ELIZABETH HOLMES

Take the case of Elizabeth Holmes, the founder of Theranos. Holmes built her company on bold claims of revolutionizing blood-testing technology, convincing investors, board members, and employees that she was on the verge of changing the world. However, as we now know, the technology never worked as promised. Holmes's ability to charm and manipulate those around her allowed her to continue the deception for years, all while endangering patients and defrauding investors. Her lack of remorse and her willingness to continue misleading others, even as the company collapsed, are classic psychopathic traits.

THE MANY FACES OF DARK PSYCHOLOGY IN THE WORKPLACE

Some individuals view their colleagues not as teammates working toward a common goal, but as stepping stones for personal advancement. Those with the dark traits of Machiavellianism might charm their way into promotions, play political games, or sabotage others behind the scenes.

Let's say you work with someone who always seems to take control in meetings, even though their ideas aren't necessarily better than anyone else's. They might use flattery or fake concern to gain favor with the boss, then undermine their colleagues when no one is watching. As time goes on, they take credit for group projects, shift blame when things go wrong, and manipulate relationships to climb the corporate ladder.

Here are some common personality profiles that emerge when manipulation runs rampant in the office.

The Fake Team Player

Imagine your colleague Matt is friendly and seems supportive when you first start working together. He compliments your work, suggests ideas for collaboration, and makes you feel like a valued team member. But eventually, you start noticing that Matt is increasingly taking credit for things you've done. When you bring this up, he deflects with smooth-talking excuses and makes you feel like you're overreacting. Eventually, you realize Matt is more interested in using your efforts to boost his own profile than in genuine teamwork. This is classic Machiavellianism—charming, manipulative, and focused on self-advancement. Matt isn't interested in building meaningful relationships at work; he's interested in using your expertise to elevate others' perception of his authority and power.

The Person Parading as an Expert

In today's digital world where you can easily brand yourself as an expert on social media, it's possible for anyone to exaggerate their qualifications. Some people get away with inflating their credentials because we tend to trust that they are being truthful on their website or their LinkedIn profile. If we don't take the time to verify their claims, they may succeed in deceiving us.

As someone who has been certified by the Department of Defense (DoD) as a military interrogator, I can verify that I have conducted numerous interrogations during the Global War on Terrorism. This hands-on experience has given me extensive training in interrogation and interview tactics, as well as expertise in analyzing human behavior, including body language. While you can find plenty of "body language experts" online, it's often challenging to find information about their credentials or previous work. They may assert that they have degrees, have been recognized as a top entrepreneur, or are bestselling authors, but how can we be sure that these claims are accurate? If we don't verify their assertions, we may fall into the trap of believing in frauds and scam artists. We might even trust them and invest a significant amount of our hard-earned money in their services, assuming that they are the key to our success.

Real-Life Profile: The Worker Who's Hiding Something

Years ago, I worked for a government contracting company on a military base. We were tasked with hiring another instructor for the team, and my boss handed me two résumés to review. The candidate I initially wanted ended up taking another offer, leaving us with our second choice—let's call him Al.

From the beginning, something about Al's résumé felt off. It was eleven pages long and bloated with self-congratulatory statements about routine tasks that were part of his job, such as mandatory security training that every government employee has to take. I noticed that he listed these basic requirements as "accomplishments," which struck me as an attempt to inflate his experience. Even during the interview, my gut told me something wasn't right, but the team was stretched thin, and we needed someone fast. My boss decided to hire him because, on paper, there wasn't any evidence for why we shouldn't.

Soon after Al joined, I assigned him some training sessions to lead. I gave him plenty of time to get up to speed on the material before his first class, and when the day came, I sat in to audit his performance. What happened next was one of those moments that make you cringe even in hindsight. Instead of engaging with the students or explaining the material, Al read each PowerPoint slide word for word, making no effort to teach. The students were looking at me, clearly confused and unimpressed, and I was mortified. This was someone who had claimed to be an expert, but it was obvious he had misrepresented himself.

After the class, I pulled him aside and asked why he had simply read off the slides. His response was, "I thought that's what you wanted." When I pressed him further, he gave no further explanation. He hadn't prepared, he hadn't learned the material, and despite his long-winded résumé, he didn't have the expertise he claimed. Eventually, with my boss's approval, we removed him from teaching duties, but we couldn't fire him right away. He was moved to another project, and I breathed a sigh of relief, thinking he was no longer my problem. I knew he'd lied about his qualifications, but they pulled him onto the other project regardless.

Al's new role required him to work at two different locations about forty minutes apart. He was to drive back and forth between them daily. One day his new supervisor called me looking for him. Apparently, Al hadn't shown up at the other location when he said he would, which raised a red flag. I told them he'd left at 9:00 a.m. and should be there by now. He never showed up to work that day. Because in my gut I knew Al was a liar and a fraud, I reported him as a security concern.

The next morning, he was called to a meeting with his boss. Within a week, he was fired. An investigation turned up evidence that he was stealing classified material and storing it in a warehouse. He would tell one of his work locations that he was at the other location and spend his day at the warehouse. His motive for all this deception: money. He was extremely materialistic, which made him a big spender who lived outside his means. His plan was to try to sell classified information to get out of debt.

The lesson here is clear: When something doesn't feel right in the workplace, whether hiring someone new or dealing with a questionable coworker or boss, trust your instincts and investigate it. Ignoring those gut feelings can lead to bigger problems down the line.

The Social Engineer in the Workplace

Another tool scammers and manipulators use, especially in the workplace, is social engineering. Social engineers manipulate people into divulging confidential information, often with devastating consequences. They exploit human nature—our tendency to trust, help, or avoid confrontation—and use it against us.

Social engineers are masters of dark psychology because they do their homework. They learn everything they can about the company, its employees, and internal operations. Armed with this knowledge, they can easily blend in, sometimes by doing nothing more than wearing the right clothes or knowing just enough jargon to seem legitimate. Most scammers prefer to hide behind a screen, using phishing emails or fake websites to steal information, but others pride themselves on lying to your face and getting away with it.

Real-Life Profile: The Malware Maven

Red team testing helps companies know if and how they are vulnerable to malware attacks. In one instance detailed in Computerworld.com, a security firm specialist name Chris Nickerson was able to prove to a big-time company how vulnerable they were to criminals and infiltrators. He was able to gain entry into one of their offices simply by wearing a $4 company T-shirt he bought at a thrift store. He researched the company's public info and used it to "speak the language" of the company and gain entrance. Once Nickerson entered the office, he plugged thumb drives with malware on them into random computers. He was able to hack into the network, all in plain sight of actual company employees. If this had been a ruthless social engineer, the damage could have been extensive: The company's data would have been breached, and intellectual property and employee identities would have been exposed. The entire company could have been brought down in hours.

While Nickerson had no ill intent, there are individuals who intend to do wrong and have a hunger for destruction. The thrill of deception makes them feel invincible, which fuels their manipulative behavior. When they deceive, they are focused on the reward of their deception. Because they are not worried about the consequences of their lies, they have no anxiety and can come across as confident and charismatic when lying. These types of liars are known as powerful liars—not because they are skilled at lying but because they don't exhibit the usual signs of stress that give most people away when they lie. There's no rapid blinking, no fidgeting, no noticeable rise in their voice pitch. They tend not to feel nervous or anxious when they lie, and therefore, cortisol, the stress hormone, does not get released. Instead, they're calm, composed, and often likable.

Toxic Leadership: A Case Study

Let me share another story, one that's all too familiar for many professionals working under toxic leadership. A friend of mine, a military officer, found herself in a difficult situation with her superior. Let's call my friend Jane, and the superior Karen. Jane worked hard, often arriving early and staying late. She was a team player, extroverted, and dedicated to boosting morale. But Karen, who had openly admitted she didn't trust women and favored her male colleagues, began to single Jane out.

Karen's behavior was subtle at first—favoring her male counterparts for promotions and projects—but it escalated when Jane covered for her during a work event. Karen, in a drunken state, stumbled and fell, and Jane got her up on her feet and shielded her from prying eyes. The next day, instead of showing gratitude, Karen turned on Jane. She called her into a private meeting, accusing her of being negative and lacking accountability. She reported Jane's supposed "negativity" to their superiors, effectively sabotaging her. Jane was blindsided.

This kind of manipulation is classic narcissistic behavior. Karen couldn't handle being vulnerable or indebted to Jane, so she flipped the narrative. Jane, once an enthusiastic and motivated worker, found herself withdrawing, keeping her head down, and just doing the bare minimum to avoid conflict. The workplace, which had once been a place of purpose and fulfillment, became noxious.

Jane came to me for advice, and I told her to reclaim her power. I urged her to walk into the office the next day as her full self—not the diminished version Karen had tried to create. I also advised her to document everything, from Karen's disruptive behavior to her own efforts at reconciliation. If the situation didn't improve, at least she would have the evidence to protect herself when she escalated the issue to higher-ups. After our conversation, she was ready to face Karen and work with a positive attitude. She took back control by believing in herself and prepared to hold Karen accountable. Karen eventually was counseled and Jane excelled in her role.

Narcissistic bosses like Karen thrive on control and power. They create a hostile environment where employees feel small, question their worth, and often lose their confidence. Usually, these are the people who are the most insecure. If you find yourself in a similar situation, it's critical to recognize that the problem isn't you. Toxic leaders project their insecurities onto others, using manipulation to maintain control of what they feel is a sink-or-swim environment.

The Boss Who Uses Both Flattery and Fear

Some higher-ups, the kind who thrive on power and deception, use a combination of flattery, fear, and guilt to keep employees compliant, creating a toxic work environment.

My friend Maria worked at a marketing firm where her boss, Brian, was known for being overly complimentary—when it suited him. "You're the best on the team," he would say, "I don't know what we'd do without you." At first, Maria felt appreciated, but soon she noticed that the praise always came when Brian needed something extra from her—whether it was staying late to finish a project or taking on responsibilities that weren't hers.

Whenever Maria expressed hesitation about the additional work, Brian would turn on the charm. "I just know you're the only one who can do this right," he'd say. But if Maria still resisted, Brian's tone would shift, and he'd drop phrases like, "I thought you were a team player," or "You don't want to let everyone down, do you?"

Flattery, followed by subtle threats, is a manipulative tactic that plays on both pride and fear. By building someone up with compliments, the manipulator creates a sense of loyalty and obligation. But when that person starts to push back, the manipulator quickly switches to using guilt or fear of disappointing others to regain control. Maria found herself working long hours and feeling increasingly frustrated, but Brian's manipulation kept her from confronting the situation for months. Eventually, she realized that the constant praise was just a tool to keep her compliant and overworked.

The Colleague Bent on Sabotage

Lies can be used as a form of manipulation, especially when colleagues are competing for recognition, promotions, or control. Bill, a project manager, found himself constantly at odds with his colleague, Jake. While they were supposed to be collaborating on a major project, Bill began to notice discrepancies in Jake's work. Jake would "forget" to send important emails, misrepresent facts in meetings, and even take credit for work that Bill had done. When confronted, Jake would always have an excuse—he'd claim he misunderstood, or that Bill must have misunderstood who completed which task.

But the final straw came when Bill overheard Jake spreading false rumors about him to their boss, subtly suggesting that Bill was the one missing deadlines and not pulling his weight. By distorting the truth and planting seeds of doubt, Jake was manipulating their boss into viewing Bill as unreliable, hoping to gain the upper hand in their professional rivalry.

This type of deception—sabotage by lying—is especially damaging because it undermines trust not just between the individuals involved, but within the larger team or organization. Bill eventually gathered evidence of Jake's behavior and brought it to HR, but the experience left him wary and mistrustful, a common result of being on the receiving end of workplace deception.

> ## DARK PSYCHOLOGY DEFENSIVE: STAY CALM AND USE LOGIC
>
> Manipulators thrive on emotional reactions. When you stay calm and focus on facts, it becomes harder for them to push your buttons or create doubt. If someone tries to provoke you, respond with logic and ask direct, clarifying questions like, "Can you show me where I agreed to that?" or "Where did you get that information?" This shifts the pressure back onto them to justify their actions.
>
> Another tactic is consensus—use social proof to your advantage. If you notice that the majority of your team is aligned on a project but one person keeps manipulating the situation to benefit themselves, call attention to the group consensus. Try saying, "It seems like everyone else agrees we should move forward with this approach."

The Friend Who Lies to Get Ahead

Friendships are built on trust, but deceit can destroy even the strongest bonds. Rose and Katie had been best friends since college. They supported each other through breakups, career changes, and major life events. But things began to change when they both applied for the same promotion at work.

Katie began dropping subtle hints to their boss, Mike, behind Rose's back that she didn't think Rose was fully committed to the new role. Katie knew that Rose had a better chance of getting the promotion, but she was tired of Rose always getting everything so easily. Katie wanted to win this promotion for herself. To undermine Rose's credibility, she engaged in casual conversations with Mike. During one such conversation, Katie mentioned that the new role was more of a leadership position that would demand more time and responsibility—qualities she claimed she was ready and willing to embrace. She suggested that Rose didn't want the extra pressure and was happy in her current role because it allowed her time with her family. Katie further implied to Mike, "She won't tell you that because she doesn't want to upset you or make you think she values her family over work."

By making these comments, Katie tried to appear supportive while subtly undermining Rose. When Mike approached Rose, he awkwardly indicated that if she didn't want to apply for the position, he would respect her decision. Confused, Rose asked why he thought that. He informed her that Katie had expressed those concerns because Rose wanted more flexibility in her work schedule for family time.

Feeling hurt and angry, Rose confronted Katie about it. Katie denied everything, claiming, "I would never say that about you! He must have misunderstood me. I know you want that role and you would be perfect!"

Katie intentionally lied to damage Rose's chances of getting the promotion. By sowing seeds of doubt in the boss's mind while pretending to support Rose, Katie attempted to manipulate the situation for her own benefit. Despite the betrayal, Rose applied for the position and ultimately got the job. As a result, her friendship with Katie ended, and Rose could never trust her again.

REAL-LIFE DARK PSYCHOLOGY: FEAR, POWER, AND AL-QAEDA

Workplace betrayals can take even more extreme and deadly forms. It was 2003, and the United States was at war with Afghanistan. My husband was deployed and stationed in Kabul at the U.S. Embassy in charge of the Anti-Terrorism Intelligence Cell. It was a typical practice to hire local nationals, after a screening process, to work on a coalition base in the region. One local national, we will call him Azim, worked in a badging office. He was in charge of creating badges for people who needed access to the base. Through the intelligence channels, my husband was told by Army Special Forces that other local nationals working on that base were pointing the finger at Azim, saying he was bad and not to trust him. With mounting evidence, Azim was questioned.

After hours of being interviewed, Azim finally broke and admitted to the U.S. interrogators that he had been making badges for terrorist members so they could gain access to the coalition base to carry out an attack on the president of Afghanistan and the visiting U.S. ambassador later that week. Luckily, the plot was foiled. When Azim was asked why he was doing this, he said that he was being coerced by Al-Qaeda and the Taliban, and that if he didn't go along with what they wanted him to do, they would kill him and his family. These threats overrode Azim's rational thinking. While Azim saw the good that the U.S. and other foreigners were doing in Afghanistan for the people there, the mental manipulation of the terrorists and the threat to his family's safety won out. Terrorists, just like leaders of cults and gangs, use threats (a very overt form of dark psychology) to get people to comply with their demands.

THE DARK PSYCHOLOGY STOPLIGHT

Use this quiz as one indicator of whether dark psychology is present in your relationship. Answer the multiple-choice questions (or at least the ones that are applicable to your relationship) without overthinking them.

1. How does the person treat you when you have difficult or uncomfortable news to share with them? They...

    a. listen first and wait to speak, so sharing the news is easy.

    b. listen but interrupt so it takes longer to share the news.

    c. don't listen because they can't deal with it right now.

2. When you provide constructive feedback, they...

    a. listen with the intent of understanding, without getting angry or defensive. They may get irritated or angry, but they try to control it.

    b. listen, but with the intent of replying or defending themselves rather than understanding first.

    c. don't listen, call you crazy, and immediately turn the discussion to everything wrong about you.

3. When you voice a concern about a specific behavior you observed and are uncomfortable with, they...

    a. immediately take responsibility for their behavior and do not blame you for it.

    b. may not blame you fully for their behavior, but will get defensive and try to justify it.

    c. refuse to listen to you and blame you for their behavior.

4. When you confront them with actual, observable evidence that catches them in the act (of cheating or lying), they...

    a. own up to it and are willing to talk about their actions.

    b. sort of own up to it, but provide multiple excuses and beg for forgiveness, saying they will never do it again.

    c. do not own up to it and say you are irrational or crazy.

5. How would you describe your relationship?

    a. Mutually respectful most of the time.

    b. They are respectful sometimes, but not as much as you'd like.

    c. One-sided: The person wants respect but doesn't give it.

6. How do they act around your friends and family?

    a. They are considerate, allowing you to spend as much time as you want with them, and never complain.

    b. They allow you time to spend with them, but might tell you, without anger or guilt, that you spend too much time with them.

    c. They complain that you spend too much time with them—even when you try not to because you're worried about their retaliation, and they like to make you feel guilty for abandoning them.

7. When you suggest that you should seek counseling or help to be better partners, they...

    a. listen and agree because they want to be better.

    b. listen, but may not agree immediately because they aren't sure they need improvement.

    c. dismiss your suggestion immediately and say they do not need to get better; you do, and you can go to counseling.

8. When it comes to keeping a commitment to improving your relationship, they ...

    a. keep the commitment without falter.

    b. commit half-heartedly.

    c. will not commit.

9. How do they feel when you get a win (promotion, raise, award, new opportunity, money, recognition)?

    a. They are always the first to congratulate you and celebrate you.

    b. They congratulate you if they believe the "win" is worthy, regardless of how you feel about it.

    c. They don't congratulate you or celebrate you; they put you down and act jealous.

IS IT DARK PSYCHOLOGY?

Determine which letter you answered most, and find it in the key below. Note: No matter what the results are, always trust your gut feeling about a relationship.

a. Green Light

Your answers indicate that this person respects you as a family member, partner, or co-worker and supports you. You can most likely count on them and feel safe with them. They do not seem to want to cause you harm.

b. Yellow Light

This person seems to care for you, but in a conditional way. You may need to work on communicating better with one another if you want the relationship to become more of a positive force in your life. You may also need to set new boundaries. Seek an unbiased mediator or counseling. If you feel safe with this person, you may be able to resolve your issues.

c. Red Light

This person probably cares more about themselves than you. There are warning signs of dark psychology in this relationship: They make unjust demands on you. They keep you from your friends and family. They create a toxic environment that may lead you to feel anxiety, self-doubt, worry, guilt, or depression. You need to ask yourself why you are still in this relationship. How is it benefiting and rewarding you? Do you feel safe?

13 POWER MOVES TO FIGHT BACK

THROUGH EXTENSIVE LEADERSHIP TRAINING and the privilege of teaching senior government leaders for years, it became clear to me that there were proven techniques for maintaining the upper hand in every situation. These techniques are even more crucial when we're dealing with manipulation and lies. My job as an interrogator in Camp Delta after 9/11 required me to control the narrative, persuade the detainees to be honest, stay firm and resilient when times got tough, trust my gut, and validate those gut feelings by analyzing behavioral indicators. I became skilled in holding others accountable for what they did, and I learned to stay confident every minute by stepping into my power. This balance of empathy and authority that I relied on as a professional interrogator became the basis of the 13 Power Moves I developed. These are power moves that I use in my own life, whether I'm navigating an interrogation or getting to the truth in a professional or personal relationship. My approach consists of thirteen techniques that can be used in any sequence. Why so many? Because different situations require different techniques. It's for you to determine which is appropriate for your situation.

Now that you've learned, to recognize dark psychology in action, it's time to learn to face our abusers. We need to stand up and speak up against their cruel intentions. I've always believed in a quid-pro-quo relationship: You get what you give. Abusive and manipulative people don't deserve to get our consideration or respect when they don't offer their own. We need to let them know we are stronger than their pathetic ploys to gaslight or smokescreen us, threaten or coerce us. But we first need to believe that we have the courage to face our abusers. We need to know that we deserve better, and we need to be ready to seek support as we shift the power dynamic back in our favor.

Unfortunately, overcoming our fears so that we can fight is not as easy as it sounds. We've all been held back by fear of the unknown. Maybe we're afraid of being fired from a job, losing a friend when we confront them on an issue, or inviting a new person into our life. We may be afraid to open our heart to someone new because it has been broken many times before. We will always have to manage those feelings. They're a survival mechanism, a stress-response system that causes physiological reactions to keep the body functioning during flight or fight. Without fear, we could not protect ourselves from legitimate threats. The only way to handle fear of the unknown is to investigate the unknown with courage and confidence. That may look like taking that risk at work and seeing where it lands you, confronting a friend and trusting that your relationship will weather any storm, or inviting someone into your life knowing that they might break your heart.

Many of us are hesitant to have uncomfortable conversations or talks that we know may lead to a fight. But equipped with the communication techniques in the following chapters, you'll feel empowered to have clear and effective discussions. Having the courage to initiate these conversations will pay off. They will help you identify a threat (detect strange behavior), investigate it (using research, questioning, and conversational techniques), and know whether to call out a person's inappropriate behavior or run from it.

You have to show up, stand up, and speak up to stay safe from dark psychology. This is a journey, and there is no going backward. You may experience setbacks along the way, but in the end, you will know how to protect yourself and covertly influence manipulative people so you can stay safe. Are you ready to build up your armor? Here are the 13 Power Moves to protect yourself from dark psychology.

1. Trust Your Gut: Increase your awareness of deceptive, cunning, and manipulative behaviors by identifying and trusting your gut feeling. We all pick up on subtle red flags or behavioral indicators, whether it's a facial micro-expression of emotion or an incongruent shoulder shrug. The trick is not to push them out of your mind but to follow them where they lead.

2. Investigate It: Go on a discovery mission and ask specific questions to acquire the information you need to catch a liar. I will share my go-to lie-exposing questions and walk you through scenarios to avoid being scammed by a liar.

3. Hold Them Accountable: Those who want to cause us harm need to be held accountable for their words and behaviors. By using specific phrases I've tested for over two decades of work in interrogation and interviews, you can persuade liars to tell the truth and own up to their actions.

4. Avoid Flytraps: Manipulators will try to bait you, so you'll need to figure out what's being used as bait (and avoid falling for it). If something sounds too good to be true, it probably is.

5. Covertly Influence Manipulators: There are proven techniques for persuading people to want to be honest and steering them toward doing the right thing. These tactics are so powerful that I have had criminals thank me after confessing to crimes even though their confession would land them in prison.

6. Control the Narrative: I will teach you how to run the conversation using embedded commands and elicitation techniques. Spies have been using these effective techniques for centuries. I used them to gather intelligence information from detainees (without their even knowing what information I was after). You can use them to get honest answers and decide whether to trust someone.

7. Step Into Your Power: I will tell you how to change your brain's chemistry and gain confidence in your ability to be firm, resist compromise, and avoid doubting yourself. Some of this boils down to saying "no" rather than "maybe."

8. Turn the Tables: Do and say the unexpected. Once you figure out what is most important to your manipulator, take it away.

9. Set Boundaries: Build sturdy boundaries and stick to them.

10. Create Distance: Learn to stop engaging with someone using dark psychology against you so that you can avoid sinking deeper into their trap.

11. Walk Away: Leave the person or the situation for good. Cut ties with them and learn to focus on the future, not the past.

12. Get Support: We often don't think of this as a way to keep ourselves safe, but creating a network of supporters, coaches, and mentors is paramount. I will discuss how and why.

13. Be Resilient: Learn powerful tools for "bouncing forward" (not back) from the effects of dark psychology.

9

#1 TRUST YOUR GUT AND #2 INVESTIGATE IT

YOUR BRAIN AND YOUR GUT ARE VERY CLOSELY CONNECTED. The relationship between the two is responsible for our intuitive thinking. The limbic system, our emotional center in the brain, produces our gut feeling. Because the limbic system reacts to stimuli in real time, it is also referred to as the honest brain. The other part of our brain, the unemotional, rational part, is the prefrontal cortex. It allows us to analyze and research the information we are taking in rather than just reacting to it emotionally. The limbic system, a more automatic response, can protect us from danger: If we had to analyze outside stimuli every time someone was about to strike us, we would not be able to instinctively react and get out of the way.

WHY YOU SHOULD TRUST YOUR GUT

The enteric nervous system (ENS) is a neural network inside your GI tract. Scientists believe that the ENS is an extension of your limbic brain connected to your gut by the vagus nerve in your parasympathetic nervous system, which controls things such as your immune system, heart rate, and digestion. Consider this: Your stomach lining has hundreds of millions of brain cells in it—or neurons that release neurotransmitters—and acts like a second brain. The limbic system in your brain communicates with your ENS in your GI tract. Those messages are traveling back and forth all the time, giving you feelings deep in your gut and emotional responses based on a rational reason. Knowing this, it makes sense to trust your gut feelings.

A gut feeling often stems from a signal or behavior you pick up on that doesn't match your past experience. For example, you may get a gut feeling that someone isn't being honest with you because they do or say something that doesn't line up with the typical behavior of an honest person. When what you are observing does not consciously make sense, you feel this in your gut before the signal travels to the brain. All of this happens unconsciously, so while these feelings are coming up, your conscious brain wants to pump the breaks and say, *Wait! I don't understand why I feel this, so give me time to work out the reasoning.* Unfortunately, during this time of confusion, we usually end up dismissing our gut feeling because we can't make sense of it.

There have been plenty of times in my own personal life when an instinctive feeling about someone led me to the right conclusion and told me not to trust a person. In Chapter 7, I told you about Al, the worker hiding something. I had a gut feeling that he was lying about his credentials and up to no good. He would go unaccounted for throughout the workweek and failed miserably at delivering a class because he had no instructor experience. Sure enough, he was fired and investigated for stealing classified information.

Because I catch liars and criminals all the time in my line of work, I often have gut feelings that later turn out to be based on factual evidence. I had an instinct about baseball player Alex Rodriguez lying about taking steroids. I wasn't surprised when he eventually admitted in an ESPN interview that he had taken performance-enhancing drugs. I also knew that cycling champion Lance Armstrong and politician Anthony Weiner were lying long before the truth came out publicly. If you're having a gut feeling, trust it, but before you jump the gun and label someone a liar, be sure to investigate that feeling.

LOOK FOR INCONGRUENCE

If your gut is telling you that something is wrong, check your theory. When people are honest, their verbal and nonverbal behaviors match. We call this behavioral congruence. When they're lying, you'll note a discrepancy. When you see incongruent behaviors in someone, it's a red flag. Do not trust them. Instead, evaluate them and get as much information as you can about the person and the situation.

Behavioral incongruence is a key indicator of deceit and dark psychology, because before someone speaks a lie, the truthful thought appears first in their brain and is reflected in their body language and facial expression. Even as they are lying, their body can be a more accurate indicator of how they really feel. Look for facial and body language clues to investigate whether your instincts about a person are correct.

Incongruent Head Shaking

In most cultures, if I answer yes to your question, I should nod in congruence; if I answer no I should be shaking my head from side to side. But let's say I respond to your yes-or-no question with, "Yes, absolutely, 100 percent of the time" and I shake my head from side to side. I am acting in an incongruent manner. Truthful people tend to be in sync; liars are mismatched. I say "tend to" because, in the world of deceptive analysis, nothing is 100 percent accurate.

Shoulder Shrugs

Shoulder shrugs are a universal sign of uncertainty. So if I say, "I don't know what to think about your behavior" and I shrug my shoulders, that makes sense because my body language is congruent with the words that I am saying and how I'm really feeling. If your first date says to you, "I'd like to go out again sometime," and they shrug their shoulders, you most likely will *not* get a second date with this person. Of course, if someone has a shoulder injury, this may influence their shoulder movements. But if they don't, and they say, "I know exactly what happened" as they shrug their shoulders, you have a problem. They are doubting what they are saying—and so should you.

The Backslide

Have you ever been talking to someone, and then suddenly they take a step backward? Or have you ever seen a speaker move

EMBELLISHED RESPONSES

An embellished response can often indicate deception. Truth tellers typically have no problem answering closed-ended yes or no questions with a straightforward "yes" or "no." In contrast, liars often feel the need to convince us of their lies, resulting in overly detailed responses to simple questions. They may provide unnecessarily lengthy explanations or use defensive tactics. Additionally, they may use their body language to convince you of their lie by enthusiastically nodding or shaking their head.

away from their audience during their lecture? This is a body language tell, or cue, that sometimes indicates that a person is uncomfortable and wants to create more space between themselves and their audience. They might have lost their train of thought or become self-conscious or worried.

Has there ever been a time when you were introduced to someone and they suddenly leaned back while meeting you? They probably didn't create that distance for no reason. A thought they had made them want to increase the space between you. If you experience people increasing their physical distance from you, it could be for many reasons: Did you do or say something to make that person uncomfortable or embarrassed? Are they nervous you'll ask them a question they don't want to answer, or are they just intimidated by you? Maybe you unknowingly took a step forward and violated their personal space. Maybe it's the onions you ate for lunch or the cigarette you smoked. Or perhaps that person just wanted to leave the conversation and they were starting to make their getaway by stepping away from you. Whatever the reason, that person is saying with their body language, *I don't want to be this close to you anymore.*

Backstepping is never a good thing; it indicates that a person is uncomfortable, has lost confidence in themselves, or wants out of a conversation or situation. If you are questioning someone on their behavior and they back away from you, be aware that they *do not* want to have that conversation. Your job is to figure out why.

Hand Motions and Face Touching

Hands reveal a lot about how a person feels and whether or not they are being honest. Hands are used by manipulative people to hide facial expressions like anger, disgust, or ill-timed happiness (like smiling or laughing at a funeral). They can also reveal fear, like when we use our hands to cover our neck, a particularly vulnerable zone for humans. Here are some proven ways to interpret the hand gestures of others:

Hand to neck: Hands to the front of the neck may indicate that a person is uncomfortable, worried, or fearful. Hands on the back of the neck can be a sign of stress or discomfort. This is a pacifying or self-soothing gesture instinctively used to ease the tension from your neck muscles caused by stress or discomfort. Because most people are uncomfortable when they lie, this move suggests that deception is afoot. It can also be a way of saying, *You're a pain in my neck.*

POWER ZONES

The body has three power zones, areas that protect vital organs and regions of the body: the neck dimple (suprasternal notch), the belly button, and the groin. If someone struck us in any of these three areas, we could suffer serious health consequences. So when we feel threatened in any way (a stranger approaches us, a dog lunges at us, an insult is hurled at us, or an audience intimidates us), we cover these areas subconsciously to protect our health.

Some individuals reflexively cross their arms in front of their stomachs, while others clench their hands in front of their groin. Covering any of the power zones is a tell. It reveals our insecurity and makes us appear weak. The act of covering up our power zones also makes us feel more insecure. If someone in your life is so threatening that you find yourself covering these zones often in their presence, it could be an indicator of dark psychology.

POWER POSES

In a paper published in *Psychological Science* and co-authored by social psychologist and Harvard professor Amy Cuddy, hormone levels of 42 male and female research subjects were measured 17 minutes after they were placed in either high-power or low-power poses for a one-minute duration. Researchers concluded that spending a short amount of time in high-power poses caused testosterone to rise by 19 percent and cortisol to decrease by 25 percent. In comparison, low-power poses increased cortisol by about 17 percent and decreased testosterone by about 10 percent. The high-power poses (leaning back in your chair or standing with your hands on your hips) led to increased feelings of power and a higher tolerance for risk (Carney, Cuddy, and Yap, 2010).

Hand to face: When we feel anxious or worried, cortisol is released into the body, causing blood to rush through the system and to our face, which can make our skin—especially our nose—itch. Blood also tends to pool at the tip of the nose during stress, which contributes to the urge to swipe at it. When people touch their faces, it can indicate a sense of unease. Research has shown that the temperature around the nose and the inner corners of the eyes often rises when someone is lying. Some people also caress their chins or rub the area above their upper lip when they are being untruthful.

Hand to mouth: Touching a hand to their mouth can be a sign that a person does not want to communicate openly. The person might be holding back or stifling their words because they're doubting what another person is saying or because they don't believe it's in their interest to speak. Sometimes people will unwittingly cover their mouths as they lie or when they don't want to answer a question truthfully (almost as though they are keeping the truth inside them).

Hand to chin: This can be a sign that a person wants to be seen as powerful. It can also indicate that someone is bored, contemplating a thought, or suspicious of what they are hearing or observing. We see this gesture a lot in politicians.

Open and Closed Palms: When people show you their palms and they are outstretched facing toward you, that is a good sign that person is being truthful. They are saying, *Look! I have nothing to hide!* When people hide their palms or face them inward, that is a good sign that they are not being truthful. They are holding something (truthful information) close to themselves and refusing to share it.

Macroexpressions and Microexpressions

Dr. Paul Ekman, American psychologist and professor emeritus at the University of California, San Francisco, conducted field research to investigate facial expressions and found that facial expressions of emotions are universal. That means it doesn't matter what your ethnic background is or where in the world you were born; we all express emotions the same way. He also said that there are two ways emotions appear on the face: in a macroexpression or a microexpression. Both macro- and micro-expressions can express genuine emotions. The difference is that a macroexpression appears on the face for a second or two, and a microexpression appears for a fraction of a second. Microex-pressions are more subtle and hard to spot because they appear in a flash. Why is it important to know the difference? Liars can often conceal their true emotions, but sometimes how they really feel shows up in their microexpression. For example, if you ask your partner, "How do you feel about having children and starting a family?" and they say with a smile on their face, "Yeah, I have always wanted a big family," but you note a look of disgust flash across their face, they may be lying to you.

Here are some examples of how specific emotions express themselves on faces:

Contempt

This expression is the most dangerous because it is often mistaken for a welcoming expression when it is the opposite. Contempt is expressed only in the mouth, as a half-smile or smirk. When only one corner of the mouth upturns, and one apple of the cheek protrudes, that person is expressing a sense of moral superiority. If you see a smirk or half-smile on someone's face, do not be fooled into thinking that person likes you—they are actually thinking highly of themselves. It also doesn't mean they are lying unless it's incongruent with what they're saying. If your coworker boasts about how awesome they are or brags about getting a raise or promotion while they smirk, then their behavior is congruent. If they are complimenting you but you see that same smirk on their face, you should probably question their sincerity. Sometimes a smirk indicates a liar enjoying how well-crafted their lie is or how easily they're getting away with deception.

Anger

There are several nonverbal signals that indicate when a person is angry. Often, liars will feel angry for a few reasons: Either they may feel you are onto them or, because lying is a lot of work and mentally exhausting, they may feel challenged and uncomfortable. They might also be irritated that you don't believe their lie. To see genuine anger, look for these indicators (some will appear independently of each other): flared nostrils, pursed lips, narrowed eyes, furrowed eyebrows, or a clenched jaw. If someone says they are not angry while exhibiting any of these behaviors, they may be lying to you.

Pay special attention to instances when you see the expression of anger but it is incongruent with the person's words. For example, your boyfriend says it's fine that you're going on a girl's trip without him, but his facial expression leaks anger. Maybe your employee says they don't mind being moved to a new location, but you detect a microexpression of anger on their face: that's incongruence.

Disgust

When a person sees, smells, senses, or touches something repulsive, they usually scrunch up their nose, so you see lines at the bridge of the nose and curling of their upper lip. You may see disgust in both the nose scrunch and the upper lip, or you may see it in just one of those places. Sometimes people try to hide their disgust by controlling their nose scrunching, but their upper lip will still roll upward. When you see either of these reactions on someone's face, even if they're saying they like something, they don't.

Tension and Stress

My friend and colleague, Janine Driver, has a rule when it comes to facial expressions: "When we don't like what we see and hear, our lips disappear." When we feel angry or tense, we purse our lips. When lips disappear entirely as though the person has sucked them in, it signifies stress and discomfort. It's as if we are closing their mouth to not allow any more stress inside us. Sometimes people will gently hold their lips together as if holding the words in their mouth until they are ready to be released.

If someone bites their lip, this can also suggest tension or stress. In abusive relationships, victims sometimes pick up on the pursed lips of their abuser right before they strike. In that instance, it can be a warning of danger to come.

Doubt

Doubt can manifest as two deep lines (like a number eleven) that form when the eyebrows come together. The corners of the mouth might also droop down in an exaggerated way. This is called the mouth shrug. Much like a shoulder shrug, this can signify that a person is doubting what they themselves are hearing or they don't fully believe in what they are saying. It means *I don't know, I don't trust the words coming out of my mouth,* or *I don't trust what I am hearing.* If you see this facial expression, your job is to figure out whether their doubt is congruent or incongruent with what they are saying.

When you get a gut feeling about someone's dishonesty, study their facial expressions and body language and look for any incongruence with their words. Are they in sync or are they mismatched? Did that person leak an incongruent shoulder shrug when they said they would never lie to you? Did you see an incongruent facial expression of contempt after they said they would never hurt you? Did they show disgust when they said they were happy they met you? Did their lips disappear as you asked them where they were last night? Pay very close attention to what they are saying and dissect every word. If there is one thing I can say for certain based on years of experience in detecting truth and deception, it is that people use words on purpose— even without being fully aware of doing so. This means that the truth leaks out every time. Hold them accountable by asking them pinpointed, specific questions to get the truth.

THE GOLDEN RULES FOR INVESTIGATING DARK PSYCHOLOGY

When you are learning to play the piano or trying to memorize a speech, repetition allows you to retain the information. With each attempt, you get better. The same principle works for accurately analyzing human behavior. The more often you notice truthful and deceptive behaviors (both verbal and nonverbal) emerge when you're dealing with other people or confronting them, the better you become at noticing them. This is especially true of facial microexpressions. Decades of experience have taught me these three golden rules:

1. Resist looking only for deceptive behaviors. If you do, that's all you'll see. Remain objective and look for both truthful *and* deceptive behaviors.

2. Remember that liars and truth tellers think different thoughts. When most people lie, they are thinking, *Does my lie sound believable enough? What if I can't remember the lie? What will happen if I get caught in a lie?* Those thoughts create stress and anxiety, which leads to sweating, shortness of breath, rapid heartbeat, shaking, and dry mouth and eyes. When people become extremely nervous and stressed, they slip into cognitive overload, and the working memory part of the brain begins to shut down. Looking for signs of that shutdown is a clever way to investigate a gut feeling that someone is lying.

3. Use the critical tool of baselining to accurately detect deceit. It allows you to get an accurate read on how a person acts and speaks when relaxed. Most people experience negative emotions when they lie, which means they are not relaxed. If you know a person's relaxed behavioral patterns well, then you should be able to identify when those behaviors change, even if they're only slightly different.

Keep in mind that a person's behavior changes when they become stressed and when they lie, but stress and lying won't *always* occur synonymously. Most liars are nervous and anxious, but those with dark psychological traits are not. And then there are people who look and act very nervous but are telling the truth. If you take notice of a person's baseline behaviors and you are able to identify whether their verbal and nonverbal behaviors are congruent or incongruent, you will become a good lie detector.

HOW TO BASELINE A PERSON'S BODY LANGUAGE

In order to baseline a person's body language, you must take note of the following. You may even want to record what you notice so that you can refer back to it:

- How do they move? Observe how they normally sit, walk, talk, and gesture (with hands and facial expressions). Are they more relaxed or fidgety?

- What is their posture? Do they stand and sit with their back straight or slouched? Are their arms open and are they comfortable enough to take up space, or do they make their bodies smaller and take up less space? Is their chin held high, or is it tucked in and covering the suprasternal notch (the neck dimple)?

- Are they talkative or quiet?

- Do they lean in or lean away?

- Do they naturally avoid eye contact, or do they give it?

- Do they self-soothe with pacifying gestures such as rubbing their hands, arms, and legs or covering their necks? Do they caress their lips or keep their arms folded tightly against their body?

HOW TO BASELINE A PERSON'S SPEECH

Here are a few cues to look for when determining someone's normal speech rate and habits. Consider the following points of evaluation when confronted with someone who may or may not be using dark psychology and manipulation:

- How quickly or slowly do they speak? In my years of detecting deception, I have noticed that when people lie, their rate of speech changes. It will either increase or decrease while they lie.

- What is the usual pitch of their speaking voice? If the pitch gets higher, it may be due to stress, and that stress might come from the vocal cords tightening when they lie.

- Do they normally pause, hesitate, stutter, or use filler words when they speak? When someone is lying, they expend extra cognitive energy, which makes it difficult for them to remember the details of their untruth. As they become more anxious, they may lose cognitive control from the effort of shifting from their prefrontal cortex to their limbic brain. Typically, you will observe that the duration and frequency of hesitations, stalls, stutters, and filler words increase as they struggle to maintain their narrative. However, if you notice that a person naturally uses a lot of filler words, such as "um" and "uh," that is their baseline behavior, so it may not indicate deception or nervousness.

COGNITIVE LOAD AND LYING

Cognitive load refers to the total amount of mental effort used in working memory, the part of our brain that is constantly processing information. Working memory creates memory schemas that get transferred to long-term memory. We bring these memory

> ## THE BREATH AS A CLUE
>
> When someone is lying to you, they may begin to breathe heavily, and you will hear this in their speech. They may be out of breath because their heart rate has increased due to the fight-or-flight impulse and the stress of potentially being caught in a lie. If they haven't just exerted themselves physically and they become breathy as you dig deeper into a conversation with them, it could indicate cortisol release and the stress they're feeling as they lie.

schemas from our long-term memory to our working memory to help us understand things. Without this memory banking system, we would constantly forget what a stop sign meant.

Here's how the cognitive process applies to the act of lying: When we lie, we retrieve memory bits from our semantic memory (our memory of generalized information rather than our memory of actual experiences), and we must string those bits together to create a story that never actually happened. That takes a lot of mental effort, especially when we're being asked to recall dates and times and other specific information that has to be fabricated. Another way to look at it is that lies cannot be created from nothing. Liars must invent the details using thought and random knowledge stored in their semantic memory. This is why liars struggle to create and remember their lies. If the stress becomes overwhelming, liars may experience cognitive overload, the point when their working memory becomes overburdened from trying to pull and assemble random bits of information from their semantic memory to construct a lie. When cognitive overload occurs, mental agility starts to shut down and tasks as simple as listening become difficult. The person may fall apart from this stress. I call it "going limbic." It's when a person has become so consumed with negative emotions that they zone out.

Truth tellers have it easier because they draw upon memory traces of actual events from their episodic memory, their autobiographical memory from their life experiences. Even so, as time passes, those truthful memory bits will start to fade, making it difficult for someone to remember specific dates and times even when they are telling the truth.

So how can you tell if someone is struggling to handle complex thinking because they're building a lie? Here are some clues that a liar has reached cognitive overload:

- They mix up details or forget them altogether.
- Their speech slows down and they say less.
- They use smaller, simpler words.
- Their sentences become shorter.
- Feelings and emotions that would normally be attached to the story they're telling are not a part of the story.
- They don't hear you ask a question. Their attention goes inward instead of outward and they appear to zone out.
- They become physically ill from the stress. I have witnessed this in some of my interrogations. First the detainee starts to slow down, then they talk less, then they tune me out. Shortly after, I hear, "I do not feel well" or "I feel sick."

ANGER AND LYING

In my experience, a liar will typically exhibit anger at some point while trying to defend their lie. They'll likely have negative emotions from the start about having to lie, and then they must work to defend their lie and answer questions to which they

THE TRUTH ABOUT POLYGRAPH TESTS

Polygraph machines detect stress, not deception. They can only measure physiological responses in the body under stress, such as heart rate, blood pressure, and sweating. The machine baselines someone's nervousness (most people become nervous even when telling the truth during a polygraph test) so it can detect a change in the level of anxiety. It's used as a lie detector under the assumption that everyone gets nervous when they lie, but the problem is that not everyone does.

A polygraph is a great tool to use on "regular" liars who experience negative emotions when they lie, such as guilt, shame, embarrassment, and worry. Their limbic system responds to lying with anxiety, which a polygraph test can easily detect. But when a person such as a narcissist or a psychopath lies for pleasure (as we know they do) or for their own benefit, there is no stress reaction. They are not worried about lying and the consequences; they are focused on the reward of the lie.

It should also be noted that the brain can adapt to dishonesty, so the more dishonest someone becomes, the easier it is for them to be dishonest and the less stressful. The constant embellishment performed by the pathological liar desensitizes their limbic system to the anxiety of lying, so they don't always fail a polygraph test.

don't have the answers. There are certain behaviors people exhibit when they become frustrated with their own deception. When a liar becomes hostile, (think of politician Anthony Weiner lying about whether he sent a picture of his private parts to someone other than his wife), they may:

- Point their index finger at you (an aggressive gesture that shows they want to take control or pin you down)
- Raise their voice
- Narrow their eyes
- Clench their jaw
- Tick their tongue out (partially, not overtly) in opposition or dislike

THE BEST QUESTIONS FOR CATCHING A LIAR

Years ago, I discovered four kinds of questions that elicit very different responses from liars versus truth tellers. These are my gut-check questions—my go-to lie exposers. I ask them in the middle of an interview and again at the very end. Judging by the responses to these four questions, I can usually tell whether or not a person has lied to me. These questions haven't failed me yet, and they won't fail you.

1. **A yes-or-no question.** I ask a yes or no question during interviews in order to validate someone's truthfulness. I look for a few things: First, did the person avoid answering the closed-ended question? Avoiding answering a question, especially a simple and clear yes-or-no question, can indicate that someone is being deceitful. I'll also try asking, "Did you lie to me?" A person who hasn't lied to me should answer me with a resounding no with no added explanation. I look for whether or not they have a congruent head shake when they say no (or a nod if they say, yes). And lastly, I consider whether or not they feel the need to explain their answer or embellish it. If someone is lying to me, I notice that they often can't just say no. Instead, they will answer my closed

REAL-LIFE QUESTIONING FAIL: DEFLATEGATE

During the NFL's "Deflategate" investigation, former Patriots quarterback Tom Brady was under a lot of media scrutiny. During a CNN press conference on January 22, 2015, a reporter gave him a yes or no question: "[Deflategate] has raised a lot of uncomfortable conversations for people around this country who view you as their idol. The question they're asking themselves is, 'What's up with our hero?'" At this point in the video Brady leaked the facial expression of contempt and moral superiority. The reporter asked, "Can you answer right now: Is Tom Brady a cheater?"

Brady's response is more than a simple no. He says, "I don't believe so. I feel like I've always played within the rules. I would never do anything to break the rules. I believe in fair play and I respect the league and everything they're doing to try to create a very competitive playing field for all the NFL teams. It's a very competitive league. Every team is trying to do the best they can to win every week. I believe in fair play, and I'll always believe in that for as long as I'm playing."

He doesn't directly answer the question, but he does give us lots of information that we can analyze for deceptiveness or truthfulness. Here, it scores for deception. He said he would never do anything to break the rules. He did not say that he didn't break the rules, or better, that he didn't cheat. In statement analysis, "never" is not a substitute for "no." Also, believing in fair play and playing fairly are two different things. And who's to know if Brady believes altering footballs is considered fair play? Because he never answered the question with a no, that tells me he is trying to convince us of a lie.

ended question with a narrative explanation using noncommittal (or squishy) language. Noncommital language such as "I guess I felt offended," "I believe she said that," "It was approximately two days ago," or "I kind of hit him" is a way to avoid absolutes and accountability.

For a real-life example, in a post-trial interview with former football star O. J. Simpson in 1996, the reporter Ross Becker asked Simpson, "Did you ever have any [Bruno Magli shoes]?" Simpson paused, took a deep breath, and shrugged his shoulders as he said, "First of all, I would have never worn those ugly shoes." He intentionally did not give a yes or no answer. If he were being truthful, he would have just answered, "No."

Another famous example of dodging a yes or no question was when cyclist, Lance Armstrong was asked whether he denied the claim that in 1996, while undergoing cancer treatment, he told doctors that he had taken performance-enhancing drugs. His answer was, "One-hundred percent, absolutely," though he shook his head from side to side, indicating no. A truthful person would have answered with a simple "Yes" while giving a congruent head nod.

Liars tend to oversell a yes or no answer because they don't believe their answer is convincing enough. As a result, they might say "absolutely, always" instead of "yes" or "I would never" instead of "No."

Let's say you suspect your boyfriend is communicating with his ex-girlfriend. You ask him and he says, "I never contacted her." He's being tactical in his response and strangely specific. This clarifies that he never contacted her, but did she contact him? Let's say you ask him again and he says, "I would never reach out to her." That is a suspicious response that avoids saying whether he did reach out to her. When people say they "would never," they are referring to a future action, not answering for a past action. If he says, "I told you I would never contact her," you can follow up and investigate more by saying, "You may not in the future, but when were you last in contact with your ex-girlfriend?" I would follow-up with, "What other time?" just to get the whole picture. Keep asking until you get to the truth.

2. Why should I believe you? The second type of question is easy because there is typically only one truthful response to this question, and every other response is suspect. A truth teller will usually say, "Because I'm telling you the truth." If someone says, "Because I wouldn't lie to you," they are telling you that they wouldn't lie to you in the future, not that they haven't *already* lied to you. If they ask you in response, "Why would I lie to you?" they are evading the question which is also suspect.

3. How did that make you feel? Here is where you get to put your sensitivity to emotional cues to the test. When you ask someone this question and they are telling you the truth, they will tell you how they felt without hesitation or doubt. If they tell you they don't know how they felt, you probably caught them off guard with this question, and now they have to think of how they *should* have felt in the story they invented. Any hesitation or guesswork when answering this question is suspect. You must investigate their story more.

Consider how this might play out in your personal life. If you ask your date how they felt about your first date, they should tell you something like, "I enjoyed myself," not, "I think it was enjoyable." If you ask your spouse, "How do you feel about what I said?" and they say, "I guess I'm OK with it. I mean, I am kind of mad, but I think it's OK," don't believe them. You can't be kind of mad; either you're mad, frustrated, or upset or you're not.

4. Should the person responsible be held accountable? When you suspect a person is lying or covering up involvement in or knowledge of something, ask them this question: "Should the person responsible be held accountable or punished?" If a person has no involvement or knowledge of some wrongdoing, they will answer yes to ensure that the person who did it receives punishment. An innocent person wants to see the guilty person punished for the crime, plain and simple. Conversely, if they answer no or, more commonly, "That is not my decision to make; that is for the authorities," they may be showing leniency for the wrongdoer. The question is, why? Guilty people (whether through knowledge or association) will usually suggest a more lenient punishment because they either committed a wrongdoing or have incriminating information about it.

During the 2015 Deflategate scandal, for example, Tom Brady was asked, "If it's found that someone improperly tampered with the balls, is it important to you that someone is held accountable?" Brady answered, "*Well that's for, you know, I'm not the one that imposes, you know, those type of, you know, accountability, it's, you know, discipline, all that, that's, you know, not really my job, so....*" Anyone who teaches statement analysis will tell you that if you ask a guilty person whether or not the perpetrator should be held accountable and punished accordingly, they resist saying yes as an innocent person would. A simple yes would have been great, but unfortunately for Brady, he failed this deception-detecting question and, in my expert opinion, revealed his lie.

STATEMENT ANALYSIS FOR BEGINNERS

As a former interrogator, interviewer, body language expert, and deceptive analysis expert, I cannot accurately detect deception without analyzing words. Despite claims that most communication is nonverbal, if you were to ask me which mode of communication (verbal or nonverbal) is more accurate for detecting deception, I would say verbal. People try to control their body language, and they may have an illness or ailment that's responsible for their movements, so you really must have an accurate baseline before you analyze nonverbal communication patterns for deception. On the other hand, words give liars away every time. Paying attention to both verbal and nonverbal communication patterns offers you the most accurate answer as to whether or not someone is lying.

There are at least a hundred examples of words, pronouns, phrases, and clauses that can indicate someone is lying. People use words to communicate something, whether wittingly or unwittingly, so never take these verbal clues for granted. The truth is hidden in a person's words. If you start paying close attention to the following statement clues, you will be much closer to knowing the truth and protecting yourself from dark psychology.

Missing "I" and "My" Pronouns

By omitting or changing pronouns, people can distance themselves from a lie by avoiding taking accountability and responsibility for it. The pronouns "I" and "my" indicate that a person is taking ownership of what they say. The I-pronouns (I'm, I'll, I'd, I've) are a very good indication of honesty. Using I-words is a way for a person to acknowledge themselves and their actions and behaviors. This kind of I-word usage is common in truth tellers. When a person refuses to use "I" or "my," there is a lack of self-reference to what is being said and, therefore, we can assume that there's a lack of ownership over what's being said.

Typically, liars will replace those two pronouns—or omit them all together—with other pronouns such as "you," "we," and "they" to avoid taking ownership of knowledge or information. For example, if you ask an employee allegedly involved in

> ## ANTHONY WEINER'S PRONOUN SLIP
>
> When Anthony Weiner was lying about tweeting a lewd photo, he said, "We're trying to figure out who sent the tweet from my account." He takes responsibility for his account but not for trying to figure out who sent the tweet, because he knew he sent it. A great way to handle this statement would be to investigate it by asking open-ended questions such as, "*Who* is trying to figure this out?" and "Why aren't *you* trying to figure this out?"

an ethics violation, "What happened?" and they answer, "We're trying to figure out what happened," that is suspicious. Who is the "we"? They should have said, "*I'm* trying to figure out what happened." The employee could be avoiding responsibility, so it's worth investigating further.

Let's say you suspect your boyfriend is cheating on you. You ask him where he was last night, and he says, "We went over to Paul's to watch the game. I was home by ten." Who is *we*? If he were being honest, he would have said, "I went over to Paul's to watch the game." An "I" response shows accountability for his actions; a "we" response avoids it.

Intent But No Action

Pay attention to when a liar unknowingly tells you what they *didn't* do. I call this indication "intent but no action." If someone tells you they started, tried, or decided to do something instead of saying they did it, they may be indicating what they failed to do (or that an action never happened at all because they fabricated the story). For example, if your girlfriend says to you, "I tried to get my ex to stop calling me," she may have tried to get her ex to stop calling, but you can assume from how she worded that statement that her ex is still calling her.

Listen for the Setup Words "So" and "Well"

Two words to pay attention to, especially when they begin a sentence, are "so" *and* "well." Either of these words is a setup, a preparatory command, for heavy content to come. The content to come may be a lie, it may be something we aren't expecting to hear, or it may be something that the speaker knows will make the listener emotional. Whatever it is, you are being given a mild warning for what is about to be said.

The word "well" can be used as a stalling technique while the person figures out how to say something. The use of "well" does not always mean that a person is about to lie, but it does mean they needed an extra few seconds to think about their answer. A person using the word "well" could be about to answer truthfully knowing you will not like the truth. They might just be revealing that they are hesitant to tell you. Liars sometimes use "well" before they are about to lie, even if they are going to lie by omitting certain information instead of creating a false statement.

"Actually" and "Basically"

These two words always mean that there is more to the story. The words "actually" and "basically" both indicate that there is another thought or idea at play in their logic. It often tells us that there is more information not being said. When you hear this, it's important to follow up with questions to investigate.

For example, if you asked me, "Lena, do you enjoy writing books?" and I responded by saying, "Actually, I do," you'd be thinking, *Why did she say "actually"?* What is the other thought I am thinking? Did I lie? Did I used to not like writing but now I do?

Either way, I should have just said, "Yes." A good statement analyst would follow up and ask, "Why do you enjoy writing books?"

Let's look at a more serious example. Let's say you are online dating, and one prospect tells you that they are actually sick of dating and want to settle down. They are offering this statement in contrast to another thought they are thinking. They might have liked it initially, but now they are sick of it. You won't know unless you ask them to explain why they said "actually." The word "basically" can be handled similarly.

I introduced you to the infamous Drew Peterson in Chapter 5. Consider the words he used during an interview with ABC News's Barbara Pinto (as quoted in the November 20, 2007, ABC News article, "Ex-Cop to Missing Wife: 'Make Yourself Seen"): "I'd look at me as a bad guy. Basically, I'm a good person, and I've done good things." Note his use of the word "basically." My follow-up question would be, "When are you not a good person?" (Most likely, it's when he is abusing and murdering his wives.)

Text Bridges

Another way liars try to get away with hiding information is by using a text bridge, which is a group of words used to cover up a chunk of time and information. That missing information may be known or unknown, so a text bridge does not automatically indicate that someone is lying. It does, however, indicate that there is missing information. Here are some examples of text bridges: "all of a sudden," "suddenly," "and then," "and the next thing I remember."

For example, "I almost drowned when I was thirteen. I got knocked down by a wave, and while I was tossing and tumbling underwater, I ran out of air and took a breath. The next thing I remember is washing up on the beach, coughing up water." I used a text bridge ("the next thing I remember") that jumped over time and information because that's where the information is missing. I don't know what happened between the time I took a breath and the time I washed up on shore.

Here is another example that may be more relevant to you. Suppose your eighteen-year-old child got into a fender bender with your car. When you ask them what happened and they say, "I stopped at the stop sign, then went to go, and the next thing I remember, a car ran into me," you may want to investigate that story a little more.

Strange or Grammatically Incorrect Word Choice

Liars violate grammar rules and use words in telling and surprising ways. Consider a statement from Drew Peterson during a televised *ABC News* interview after his fourth wife, Stacy, went missing. He said, "Why would I go search for something

---

TRUE CRIME CASE STUDY: JODI ARIAS

Jodi Arias, who brutally killed her ex-boyfriend Travis Alexander in Arizona on June 4, 2008, gave a televised interview—before her conviction in 2013—where she blatantly lied to the reporter while describing the events of the morning Travis was murdered. She claimed that two masked men came in and killed him. During the interview she said, "I heard, um, a really loud, um, pop, and the next thing I remember, I was lying next to the bathtub and Travis was, um, screaming." She used a text bridge and three filler words while avoiding eye contact with the reporter as she lied. Arias stabbed Travis twenty-seven times, slit his throat, and shot him twice. That's what was going on during her text bridge.

---

who wasn't there?" He should have said, "Why would I go search for *someone* who wasn't there?" This statement reveals that he considers Stacy a thing because he knows she's dead. He smiled as he said this, not because he was happy but because he thought he was going to get away with murder.

10

#3 HOLD THEM ACCOUNTABLE AND #4 AVOID FLYTRAPS

WHEN YOU'VE TRUSTED YOUR GUT that someone is lying and you've investigated that presumption enough to feel confident that they're lying, it's time to get answers. By using specific phrases and effective questions that have worked for me in over two decades of interrogations and interviews, you can persuade liars to give you the whole truth, details and all. It's the only way to hold them accountable for their behavior. Since this approach has been tested on the worst terrorists and criminals, you can be confident that it will work on a manipulative partner, boss, friend, or family member.

QUESTIONING TECHNIQUES FOR GETTING KEY DETAILS

Most people think they are asking good questions when they aren't. Leading questions, long-winded questions, and confusing questions can all easily result in misleading responses. Sometimes questions aren't questions at all: they're comments. A question can sound accusatory in a way that shuts down the person being interrogated. Other times, it can lead them to give you the answer you want regardless of the truth. When we want factual, detailed information, we need to use the most effective questions possible.

The first rule of thumb is to make sure your questions start with an interrogative: "who," "what," "where," "when," "why," or "how." This kind of open-ended question encourages a narrative response. Unlike the yes or no question, which serves to tell you if someone is dodging the truth, open-ended questions serve to gather detailed information that you can use to check for truthfulness and accuracy.

Follow this second rule and you will be able to get the truthful information you seek: Ask for exactly what you want to know. For example, if you want to know how the person you are dating feels about committing to you and becoming exclusive, you wouldn't ask them, "What do you think about our relationship?" Although it is an interrogative question, it's too vague. If they don't want to be exclusive with you but don't want to hurt your feelings, they can easily just say that they are happy or that they see it has potential for a long-term relationship. You won't know if they want to be exclusive or not. Instead, ask "How do you feel about being an exclusive couple?" This way you get a more detailed and specific answer and find out what you want to know.

Laddering

Salespeople use probing questions (questions that begin with "why" or "how") with a technique called laddering to find out what buyers really want, to learn what will motivate them to buy, and to succesfully sell them a product based on that information. When you use laddering, it appears as though you are genuinely concerned about the other person and you're listening closely. That feeling can help foster trust and persuade someone to tell you the truth.

Let's say you're the boss and your employee comes to you and tells you they're thinking of leaving the company. They are a crucial employee with talent and potential for a future leadership role, so you don't want to lose them. Here is the conversation:

You: "Why do you want to leave?"

Employee: "I'm just not happy anymore."

You: "Why aren't you happy?"

Employee: "I don't feel challenged."

You: "Why don't you feel challenged?"

Employee: "I applied for the promotion last month, and Martin was promoted. Yet I've been here longer. I raised revenue for the company, and all of my feedback has been positive. I don't understand why I wasn't promoted. Martin hasn't raised the revenue I have and his peer review wasn't positive."

Now you know the real reason why that employee wants to leave. It is not because they don't feel challenged; it's because they wanted a promotion and felt someone else got it unfairly.

INEFFECTIVE QUESTIONING TECHNIQUES

Avoid these verbal missteps when trying to hold someone accountable, especially if you think you're the victim of dark psychology.

Vague Questions

If you ask a vague question, you will most certainly get a vague answer, especially if someone is purposely trying to deceive you. Vague questions make it easy for a person to lie by omitting truthful information. This is the easiest form of lying. You don't want to make it easy for someone to lie to you, so keep your questioning specific.

Leading Questions

Attorneys are notorious for asking leading questions, that is, they are leading a witness to an answer they want to hear. This type of question can trap someone into saying something untrue and can paint them into a corner with their response.

Imagine if you asked your partner, "You're happy in this relationship, right?" There is only one answer you're looking for, and you're making it very easy for that person to say yes even if they don't agree. Don't you want to know if they are truly happy or not? If so, ditch the closed-ended, leading question and ask, "What about our relationship makes you happy?"

Compound Questions

Lastly, avoid the common mistake of asking compound questions (two questions at once). If a person has something to hide, you've given them a free pass to answer the less-incriminating question and avoid the other one. If you make this mistake, be sure to follow up and repeat the question they didn't answer until they do.

Ask, Don't Tell

This mistake can have grave consequences. Interviewers who lack confidence in their questioning skills tend to tell people the answer instead of asking for it. Here is an example of what I mean from an interview with Casey Anthony in March 2017.

True Crime Case Study: Casey Anthony

Casey Anthony was suspected of killing her two-year-old daughter, Caylee, in 2008. On December 11, 2008, Caylee's skeletal remains were found wrapped in a blanket inside a laundry bag in the woods near Casey's parents' residence. The little girl had been missing for thirty days, a fact that Casey hid from her own parents. When her mother demanded to see her granddaughter and asked Casey where she was, Casey blamed a fictional nanny for taking her. One of Casey's friends had a nanny by the name of Zenaida Gonzales. Casey used that name in her lie regarding the whereabouts of her missing daughter. Casey's mother made her call 911 despite the fact that Casey didn't want to.

Casey continued to lie to her parents and the police. This case went to trial, with Casey being the main suspect. During the trial, Casey blamed her father for her child's death (and still does to this day). She also alleged that her father and brother sexually abused her, but both her parents passed a polygraph test in 2023 regarding Casey's accusations. Casey was acquitted of murdering her daughter, Caylee, on July 5, 2011. She has never taken a polygraph test.

As an expert in human behavior, I have no doubt that she is responsible for her daughter's death and should be spending her life behind bars for it. I will share some of my analysis of her lies and give an example of why asking effective questions to discover the truth is so important.

Reporter: To your understanding, how did she die? (referring to Casey's daughter, Caylee)

Casey: I don't know.

Reporter: You don't know? Something about drowning, possibly? *(Leading question, telling Casey the answer. He should have stopped after asking a better question like, "Why don't you know how she died?")*

Casey: Everyone has their theories. I don't know. *(She refuses to answer the question. "Everyone has their theories, does not answer the question. The reporter asked her how Caylee*

*died, not about what other people's theories are. This is a
person who wants to hide the truth.)*

Reporter: So your parents had her. *(Again, leading Casey to
an answer. The reporter should have asked, "Who had (was
with) Caylee at the time of her disappearance?")*

Casey: My dad did.

Reporter: Next thing you know, she's missing? Right? How
did it play? *(Leading question, telling Casey the answer.)*

Casey: I did what I was told. I don't remember too much of
what happened" *(This statement is not an answer, and it
doesn't even make sense. She refuses to answer the question
again. "I did what I was told," is vague. Who told her to
do what? Her daughter goes missing for a month, and then
her remains are found in a bag. This has got to be the most
traumatic experience of her life, and she doesn't remember
it? She is dodging the question, which is typical of someone
who wants to hide the truth.)*

This is a classic example of how ineffective questioning gets
you nowhere. The reporter told Casey the answers instead of asking her for them. This is not unusual for interviewers who are
trying to avoid upsetting the interviewee and risk having them get
up and leave the interview. You should never have to sacrifice
your questions for fear of losing rapport. If you have established
trust in the beginning, you should be able to ask clear, direct
questions. When you are indirect in your questioning or feed
someone the answers, you can't obtain any detailed information.

In my professional opinion, Casey was using a smokescreen
to disguise the truth that she killed her daughter, whether on
purpose or by accident. She devised a smokescreen of a childhood spent in a troubled house where her father and brother

sexually abused her and growing up learning to lie. She has dark psychological personality disorders.

KEEPING THE UPPER HAND

Controlling the conversation means you set the tone, the pace and the length, and most importantly, you choose the discussion topics. You decide what you will and won't discuss. There are three factors to be aware of when controlling a conversation: You must actively listen, you must remain calm, and you must know what to say to avoid sounding accusatory.

Ultimately, staying in control of your emotions will give you the upper hand in a conversation. This will become especially challenging when the other person is highly emotional and limbic. A conversational partner who is not emotional but who is using manipulative tactics on you is another challenge. In that case, you must be smarter than them and remain calm. When a manipulator like this wants to turn the tables on you, they may perceive you as weak. If you show up strong and confident, you may catch them off guard, and they may falter.

I developed a method to easily deflect any attempt by a manipulator to exploit you, whether for personal gain, to belittle you, or to smokescreen you. I call it A.R.R.E., for Acknowledge, Respond, Redirect, Exit.

1. Acknowledge: Acknowledge the manipulator to keep them from becoming more angry and belligerent. This doesn't mean that you have to hear them out, and it certainly doesn't mean that you have to agree with them. It means being confident and relaxed and receiving what they are telling you verbally or nonverbally. You can give them eye contact, nod and smile, and walk away. Smiles are disarming and may catch your opponent off guard. They may stop persisting. But if they do persist, you may want to respond.

2. Respond: When you respond to a manipulator's deceptive or exploitative comment, try to use one of these approaches.

- **Repeat what they said to you,** then pause. Do not say another word once you have repeated a phrase, question, or word back to your opponent. Let them be the next person to speak, or you will lose the effectiveness of this technique. For example, if your opponent says, "You can't leave me; you are nothing without me," you would simply say, "I can't leave you?"

- **Ask for clarification,** then pause. For this technique to be effective, you should not say anything after you ask for clarification. You are forcing your manipulator to be accountable for what they just said. This technique can buy you time to think of how to redirect the conversation to another topic. An example would be if your opponent said, "You think I'm cheating with everyone! You are delusional." Ask for clarification, "Describe how I am delusional."

  Another example: Your colleague, who has applied for the same position as you, tells you, "You don't want to apply for the promotion because you're too good at what you do now. We need you in this position." You can say, "I appreciate that. Tell me why exactly you think I shouldn't apply." Hold them accountable and get clarification.

  Another example would be if your partner said, "You used to take care of yourself and liked to dress up. Now it's like you don't even try to look good for me." This may be true, especially if you've had enough of them. If this is untrue, you can say, "Why do you think I don't try to look good for you?" Or you can say, "Give me two examples." Make them give you concrete examples; make them back up what they say.

- **Be vague in your response,** and do not add any information they can use as leverage against you. Using the above example, if your colleague says, "You don't want to apply for the promotion, because you're too good at what you do now. We need you in this position," you can say, "Thank you," leaving them in the dark. They will wonder if you are going to apply and be their competition. This is a great way to hold your ground and take control.

Let's say you have a nosey colleague who is always trying to determine if you make more than them. They bait you and say, "If we get a bonus this year, I will hit six figures." You could say, "Great!" and leave it at that. If they persist and ask you, "What about you?" you could say, "I don't talk about my salary with anyone. It's always a weird topic, don't you think?" Your colleague should get the hint at that point.

3. Redirect: At some point, you may need to redirect the conversation to a different topic so that you can confidently exit the conversation and not be derailed by your abuser. Listen to the last statement they make and then change the conversation to another topic. You can even redirect the conversation by asking a question about a random topic such as the venue or restaurant you are in, the weather, or the news. What you do not want to do is ignore what they say, because that will only add fuel to the fire. Then they will blame you for their unacceptable behavior.

Let's consider a conversation between a couple. We can refer to them as Brynn and Ben.

Ben lost his job and now drinks daily and emotionally

abuses Brynn. He belittles her to make himself feel better. He says to her, "The only reason they hired you is that you're hot and all the guys just want to gawk at you."

Brynn, knowing he wants to fight and continue the barrage of insults, isn't going to let him, so she is going to take control and drive this conversation by redirecting it. She could say, "Thank you, I am feeling pretty hot these days. I think it's because of my new workout routine. Do you want to work out with me?" Or "Yes, I am feeling and looking good. It's probably because I stopped drinking as much. You should consider it, too. We should diet together." That is taking back your power! Don't defend yourself, because that will strip you of your authority.

- **Bring another person into the conversation.** This technique can take the focus off you and put it on someone else. You do not want to make one of your colleagues, friends, or family members the new target of your abuser's insults, so be mindful of who you bring into the conversation. You can use this technique in one of two ways. First, if you are at an event with lots of people around you, you can pretend to see someone you know to get out of the conversation. For example, you can say, "Can you excuse me for a minute? I see someone I have been trying to talk to all day" and then walk away.

  The other way to use this technique is to bring another person into your conversation physically. This may be a bit harder because if there are no other people you know around you, you will have to bring a stranger into the conversation. Either way, you want to invite someone into your conversation to take the focus off you and onto them. You can introduce the new person to the conversation to stop your abuser's attempts at arguing with you or demanding information from you. If you are at a bar, you can wave the bartender over and say something like, "My boyfriend and I were having a debate we thought you could settle." Then ad lib. After they start talking, you can ask both inquisitive questions and redirect the conversation or devise an excuse to leave the conversation.

4. Exit: Finally, leave the conversation on your terms and timeline. You can leave the house or room, make a phone call, or go for a walk to disengage, but physically leave the area. This will give you both a cooling-off period and leaves you with the upper hand.

When you use the A.R.R.E. method, you can skillfully gain control and avoid any attempts at being sucked into a hostile conversation while still maintaining your calmness and confidence.

WHEN TO CALL THEM OUT

When it comes to mentioning the elephant in the room (that someone is lying to you), there's a proven way to get results without the person denying it and making your accusation an excuse to get defensive and angry.

If you need the truth, but you know that you will not be able to have a rational (or safe) conversation with your manipulator, do not confront them. Walk away if you can, or find support. Don't waste your time, energy, or breath on someone unwilling to communicate respectfully. Do not stay in a relationship where someone's taking advantage of you.

Assuming you feel safe to confront the liar in your life, consider your approach. If you say to someone, "You're lying," they will probably deny it instantly. Instead, you could say, "I feel there is more you want to tell me." Then wait, and avoid the temptation to say more. Leave the silence and let them be the first to break it. If you break the silence, you lose the effectiveness of this technique. If they break the silence, it might be to tell the truth.

WHY PEOPLE TELL THE TRUTH: ADDRESSING NEEDS AND MOTIVATIONS

The trick to getting someone to be honest with you is to convince them that they want to be honest. How do you do that? You find out what motivates them. Psychologist Abraham Maslow believed that human behavior is motivated by our physiological needs first, followed by our need for safety. Examples of the physiological needs are food, water, clothing, shelter, employment, and health. Once our basic needs for food, shelter, and safety are fulfilled, we climb up a ladder (Maslow's Hierarchy of Needs) to more psychological needs, such as having friendships, love, and belonging. Once that tier is fulfilled, we focus on attaining self-esteem. At the highest level is what Maslow calls self-actualization: morals, creativity, and problem-solving.

To discover what would motivate someone to tell the truth, you must first figure out what means the most to the person. Are they inward-focused on personal needs such as safety, importance, respect, embarrassment, and saving face, or are they outward-focused on food, shelter, water, being able to work, being able to earn money, taking care of family, or maintaining friendships?

To help you understand the difference between outward and inward focus, let's look at owning a car. Some people own a car for its functionality. Their main priority is a safe and reliable ride for their family. Others, want to own a luxury car that's more of a status symbol. Perhaps they want other to envy them and they want to feel special. Neither is right or wrong, but the car type fits the individual's need type.

When it comes to persuading people to be honest, consider the following questions:

- Is this person overly concerned about how others will perceive them if they are found out as a liar? This person might be tempted to tell the truth if they thought they would be admired for their honesty.

- Does this person fear losing their job, and that's why they're lying? If you can come up with a way for this person to keep their job after telling the truth, they might just tell the truth.

- Do they fear the guilt or shame that their lie has created? If so, tell them how good they will feel when they tell you the truth.

- Does this person fear losing credibility if they're exposed as a liar? Then relieve their worry and convince them that you will not expose them as a liar.

ADD VALUE TO THEIR CONFESSION

For people to open up and be honest, they must be convinced that their honesty has value. Here are examples of what you could say to address either a functional or psychological value.

Functional Value-Add: Job Security

- "If you help the company by being honest, they may be lenient with you and allow you to keep your position."

- "Until you come clean, no one will trust your work and you won't be of value to the company."

- "The company is putting a lot of effort and money into this investigation, so if it doesn't get resolved soon, they may seek legal action to avoid the effort."

- "The company considers you a risk, so they may let you go unless you help us."

- "If you tell the truth, you'll avoid getting a bad reputation. If multiple companies want to steer clear of you, where will you find work?"

Psychological Value-Add: Anxiety

- "Once you're honest, you'll feel so much better. Your stress and anxiety will go away."
- "When you communicate openly, it will reduce the fear of the unknown. We can resolve this quickly so you won't have to worry about what could happen."
- "Honesty makes you a good, moral person whom people admire and trust. You want people to trust you."
- "The company is putting a lot of effort into this investigation, which can create a negative perception of you. Your actions may cost the company its reputation, which could result in the loss of jobs for many people. How would you feel if you were responsible for others losing their jobs? You need to realize the long-reaching aftereffects of your actions on people."

Remember, never judge or blame people when persuading them to tell the truth. I was able to obtain the truth in my interrogations only by creating an environment where the other person felt safe (not judged or blamed) to tell me the ugly truth. Most people—those who do not have dark psychology personality disorders— want to be honest and truthful, but everyone is motivated by slightly different forces.

BARRIERS TO TRUTH

There are some barriers that can block your path to the truth. Unless you tear them down, it will be very difficult to get answers:

EMOTION VS. REASON IN DECISION-MAKING: A STUDY

Some people's brains are wired to make decisions based on emotion, while others make them based on reason. When communicating with someone well-versed in dark psychology, it's best to know what kind of brain you're dealing with and how they make decisions. Princeton University professor Jonathan Cohen conducted a study at the Princeton Neuroscience Institute to investigate decision-making using a functional MRI to examine how the brain works. Individuals were asked if they wanted Amazon gift certificates worth $5 to $40 now or to wait six weeks for larger-value gift certificates. The cells in the areas of the brain associated with emotion (such as the midbrain dopamine system) wanted an immediate reward. For many people, but not all, the emotion-related parts of the brain won out over the reasoning parts.

1. Ideological: The perception of no shared value system or standards of morality. If your partner sees you as different, or on the "other side," they may not want to connect with you. You will have to find common ground to persuade them to talk.

2. Social: The perception that you and your friends stand as one against them. If your boyfriend thinks you and your girlfriends are thick as thieves, then they will feel on the outside and on the defensive.

3. Emotional: The perception that negative feelings are dominant. If your friend believes you think of her as "bad" or a "cheater/liar," she may resist the negativity, and it may cloud her desire to be honest with you. People tend to dwell on negative emotions more than positive ones.

> ## HOW TO BREAK UP WITH A MANIPULATOR
>
> Do not blame or make up stories or assumptions about a manipulative partner, as this will only frustrate them, turning the conversation into an argument. Here are three tips to help you have an effective breakup conversation:
>
> **1.** Clearly state the reason(s) why you want to end the relationship. Be as objective as possible.
>
> **2.** Do not defend yourself! You have the right to how you feel. They also have a right to how they feel, so let them experience their emotions without judgment.
>
> **3.** Do not get trapped into arguing. If the other person becomes emotional, tell them you hear them, you are listening to them, but that your decision hasn't changed. Insist that they must accept your decision.

You will have to clear the air and invite positive feelings into the situation or relationship before the friend is comfortable confiding.

WHAT IS A FLYTRAP, AND HOW DO I AVOID IT?

A flytrap is a form of manipulation that traps you emotionally in the manipulator's narrative. They may bait you rationally or emotionally, but they will make it difficult for you to be free of their mind games. Let's look at some examples.

Emotional Blackmail

Emotional blackmail is the most effective kind of flytrap. It's a manipulation tactic whereby people use guilt, fear, and shame to control another person, whether it's a family member, a romantic partner, or a coworker. The manipulator creates a sense of obligation in a victim to get them to stay in a relationship.

Here are some techniques emotional blackmailers use to take advantage of someone's good nature. By exploiting your moral compass and your will to seek harmony and avoid confrontation, manipulators will try to bait you into a conversation they have scripted in advance. Why? They believe they know exactly what to say and how you will respond.

- **Offering false hope:** This is when they constantly reassure you that they will give you the one thing you want most: the love you desire, the future you hope for, and so on, but they never do. They will make you think they will by saying, "I thought you wanted to get married and start a family." or "You want to leave me? I thought we had plans to get married and start a family together." Meanwhile, they might keep cheating on you and ensuring that you don't go

---

THE MAGIC WORDS

When I want someone to tell me something important, I sometimes use this key phrasing: "I may be wrong, but I think there is more you want to tell me." Then I wait in silence and let them be the first to speak. Notice that I don't say, "I may be wrong, but I don't think you told me everything." That is accusatory and will only thwart my efforts. The goal is to avoid eliciting defensiveness, frustration, and anger. The first person to speak in this situation often loses, so don't let it be you. Usually, the person becomes uncomfortable with the silent void I create and they start speaking.

---

off birth control. They expect you to agree with what they are saying because the false promise is music to your ears.

- **Instilling fear:** They will say, "If you leave me, no one else will want you. You won't have the nice house you have now or the car. You will have nothing."

- **Guilting you:** They may guilt you out of ending a relationship with them by convincing you that you give up too quickly on things and don't see anything through in your life because you are scared of commitment.

- **Withholding praise and approval:** Until you do what they want you to, the manipulator will deny you their love or approval. Once they get you to act in the way they desire, however, they will love bomb you.

FLYTRAP INDICATORS

Here are some common phrasings that should raise a red flag and tell you you're being baited by someone:

- **You're crazy for thinking that I ...** When you're labeled as crazy by someone who you believe is manipulating you, be careful of their flytrap. This phrasing indicates that they are quick to blame everyone but themselves for the poor decisions they make. They may tell all of their friends (and yours) how crazy and unreasonable you are in order to turn everyone against you. At that point, they are (strategically) the only person in your life for you to depend on. They can do this to hold you hostage emotionally and continue to blame you for their behaviors.

- **You have no self-confidence. That's why you don't trust me.** If someone uses phrasing like this, they are willing to put you down to make themself look good. This is a dangerous flytrap that indicates an uneven power balance in your relationship.

- **All you want to do is fight with me. I'm not going to fight.** If you start to hear things like this, you might be caught in the trap of someone who's always the good person and paints you as the bad person. It's not your imagination. This is an artful dark psychological trap, so it's key that you see through it.

ESCAPE THE TRAP

If someone claims that you always fight with them, respond by saying, "A fight involves people raising their voices. Your voice is raised and mine isn't."

If they have engaged in a smear campaign against you, here's what you can do:

1. Ignore it: If these friends are your true friends, they know your character and will not believe the nonsense.

2. Address it: Have a conversation with each one individually. Begin the conversation, "It's come to my attention that my boyfriend told you I did X. I would like to tell you what really happened. I'm not defending myself, but I'm speaking up for myself, and you deserve the truth."

#5 COVERTLY INFLUENCE MANIPULATORS

LET'S TALK ABOUT HOW YOU CAN GAIN CONTROL OF A MANIPULATOR AND PERSUADE THEM to do what you want them to do, which is especially crucial if they're wreaking havoc on your life and happiness. Persuasion is all about getting people interested enough in you to believe you and follow your lead. You can't influence or persuade someone unless they believe what you are saying. Conversely, no one can influence you unless you accept their statements as truth.

American psychologist Robert Cialdini is an expert on the tools of persuasion. His six principles of persuasion represent the basic foundation of influence. Experts in dark psychology know how to work these principles in their favor.

THE SIX PRINCIPLES OF PERSUASION

1. Reciprocity: Humans feel good helping others, and usually feel obligated to return a favor.

I was an interrogator in at Camp Delta in Guantanamo Bay, Cuba in 2002. I was preparing to meet with a detainee who was a Saudi national. Up to that point my Saudi Arabian detainees were uncooperative. When this detainee came to the door of my interrogation booth, flanked on both sides by the military guards, he looked at me and I smiled. He smiled back. He quickly tried to disguise it, however. Then, instead of having the guards sit him in the uncomfortable chair, I switched his chair with mine because mine was cushioned. He was reluctant to take the nicer chair, but he did. He told me, "I want to work for you. I don't like the brothers."

Months later, he became my source inside the prison. He helped me uncover loads of valuable intelligence. He even uncovered a counterintelligence threat! When I asked him why he chose to be cooperative he said, "Because you were so nice to me the first time we met by giving me your chair that I decided I couldn't lie to you." I used the principle of reciprocity to persuade him to help me.

Consider the mail you get from nonprofit organizations asking for donations. Inside the envelopes, you might find pretty calendars, planners, or stickers. You may feel compelled to donate money to their cause because of the principle of reciprocity.

2. Commitment or consistency: This aligns with our values and our need to be consistent with who we are, and relies on the basic fact that people want to deliver on their commitments.

We are more likely to join an organization or trust someone if their core values align with our own and they consistently uphold them. People are also more likely to tell the truth if you convince them that telling the truth is consistent with their values or how others perceive them.

3. Consensus or social proof: This is the idea that if everyone else is doing something, it's probably a good idea. If people are giving hearts to a new fashion fad on social media, it makes others want to believe that they should buy into it. Before the fall of Keith Raniere, the NXIVM cult leader who sexually abused and coerced women (including minors), he had 700 followers on social media. Hollywood actresses were among some of this felon's followers before he was caught. How could that be? Because social proof persuaded people that he was an OK guy to follow. That's the dark psychology side of social proof, but we can also get a manipulative partner to behave differently if we convince them that everyone believes they're behaving badly and need to change.

4. Authority: An air of authority or expertise, or a legacy of success, is trustworthy. If you can put yourself in a position of authority or use someone with authority to help you influence your manipulator, they may be more easily persuaded to comply with your demands. This is so powerful that you have to be careful not to use it with too much force: I have seen detainees falsely admit responsibility for attacks, and I have witnessed false criminal confessions result from poor interviewing techniques by figures of authority. People tend to submit to authority figures and may go so far as to falsely confess to crimes simply to please those experts.

5. Liking: When people perceive you to be similar to them, they like you more and trust you more. From there, they can be more easily persuaded. This similar-to-me bias happens when we perceive someone to be like us, so we trust them without really knowing them.

6. Scarcity: People are easily persuaded to do something when there is urgency or a high demand. When you put an item in your cart online, it may tell you that there are only a few items of that kind remaining. If this persuades you to go ahead and buy it right then, you've been influenced by the scarcity principle.

If you state that time is running out for someone to tell you what you want to know or that they will run out of options if they don't abide by your rules, then you have leverage.

Cialdini's principles help people get what they want. If you want someone to help you, deliver on their commitment, recognize you as an authority, treat you fairly, trust you, have a calm conversation without arguing, or be honest with you, you can bend these tools to your advantage instead of falling victim to them. It may take one or all of these tactics to gain control over a toxic relationship or set healthy boundaries, but using covert influence will pay off.

WHY BE COVERT?

It's key to gain the upper hand when you're dealing with a toxic or manipulative person who believes they have you all figured out. Often, the only way to do this successfully is to do it artfully and quietly. No one likes to feel as though they're being directed, so being covert is your best chance to overthrow your manipulator without their realizing it and avoid playing the part of victim.

It's especially wise to use discreet tactics when dealing with individuals with personality disorders such as NPD. Narcissists are self-centered, irrational, and quick to defend themselves, so engaging in direct confrontation can be a losing battle. Instead of fighting with a narcissist, it's more effective to outwit them.

Introverted manipulators also tend to shy away from debates or argumentative behavior, so using a subtle approach with this type of person can help uncover the truth without being overly confrontational. When someone is relaxed and doesn't feel threatened, they are easier to influence.

THE ETHICS OF PERSUASION

You can be persistent and persuasive without delving into dark psychology yourself, but you should know where the line is.

Dark psychology is:

- Aggressively strong-arming someone into compliance
- Stating your position with the expectation that others will comply
- Only using data that supports your stance to defend yourself

Persuasion is:

- Being persistent without being pushy
- Using stats and facts to back up your beliefs or your position
- Being open to hearing someone's opinion, despite trying to convince them otherwise

COVERT MANIPULATION AT ITS WORST

Covert manipulation looks a lot different when it's a dark psychological tactic than when it's a tool for getting a manipulator to come clean. If the principles of persuasion are being used on you, there will be tell-tale signs. Manipulators will:

- Distort what you say to make themselves look better or seem like the victim.
- Play dumb and act as though they have no idea where you came up with your accusations.
- Flatter you in front of others to uphold their image as a good person, but treat you poorly in private.

KNOW WHO YOU'RE UP AGAINST

There are plenty of personality types that dabble in dark psychology, but knowing if your manipulator is type A or type B is the first step toward being successful in influencing them. If you're not sure who you're dealing with, consult the general checklists that follow, but keep in mind that everyone is a little bit of both.

Type A: The Dominant, Goal-Oriented Manipulator

Your target may be a Type A if they:

- Are competitive in nature
- Like to take charge in situations
- Are highly opinionated
- Are impatient

BODY LANGUAGE THAT GETS PEOPLE TO TALK

- Lean toward someone to make it appear you are interested in what they have to say.
- Tilt your head to one side, exposing your neck, to make it appear you are interested and contemplating what they are saying. It can also be a sign of vulnerability, which can diffuse aggression because they won't perceive you as a threat.
- Nod gently as someone is speaking; this tells them to keep talking because you are listening and interested in what they have to say.

- Get upset easily
- Prefer to speak rather than listen
- Associate self-worth with achievement
- Dislike failure
- Put intense time pressure on themselves to accomplish tasks
- Make everything urgent
- Multitask
- Enjoy taking risks
- Get frustrated with others' ambivalence
- Are determined and take the initiative
- Are tenacious and proactive
- Are a workaholic
- Have high levels of stress and worry, and the health problems that accompany both
- Are moody
- Are goal oriented rather than relationship oriented
- Like change
- Demand freedom and independence
- Are good at delegating
- Can come across as overpowering, abrupt, and insensitive
- Are motivated by money, opportunity, independence, success, leadership, or challenges

Body language to use with Type As:
- Stand tall
- Give good eye contact
- Do not cover your power zones (neck, stomach, groin)
- Take up space

Communication tactics to use with Type As:
- Think fast
- Show interest in them and what they have to say
- Praise or flatter them on one specific trait
- Speak in a deliberate and confident manner
- Own what you say
- Speak louder than normal and with more authority

How to gain a Type A's trust:
- Stand your ground
- Allow them to delegate
- Appreciate their directness and bluntness
- Be high-energy and charismatic
- Be goal oriented
- Have a growth mindset (willing to accept failure and improve)

Best persuasion tactics to use with Type As:
- Appeal to their pride and ego
- Use high, go-getter energy when pitching something to them

Don'ts for Covertly Influencing Type A Manipulators:
- Don't be wishy-washy
- Don't tell them to slow down
- Don't use filler words
- Don't smile too much
- Don't avoid eye contact
- Don't slouch
- Don't show that you care what others think
- Don't micromanage
- Don't take what they say or do personally
- Don't get easily offended by their actions

Type B: The Laid-Back Manipulator

Your target may be a Type B if they:

- Are easygoing and flexible when it comes to schedules
- Are relaxed and not easily stressed
- Are content with the status quo
- Like to dream but have difficulty initiating
- Are not very competitive
- Are friendly and charismatic
- Are relationship oriented
- Are very social
- Seek harmony in relationships
- Avoid conflict and get distressed around discord
- Tend to avoid conflict or back down from it
- Don't take work home with them
- Don't have a sense of urgency
- Are creative
- Are accommodating and accepting
- Tend to procrastinate
- Tend to look on the bright side of things
- Feel everything will eventually work out
- Get bored easily
- Have a short attention span
- Come across as unrealistic, impulsive, or whimsical

Body language to use with Type Bs:
- Angle your body toward them
- Show them your full attention
- Use smiles and nods to encourage and affirm them

Communication tactics to use with Type Bs:
- Engage in small talk
- Get to know them and express interest in them
- Laugh and bond
- Seek common ground and reinforce it

How to gain a Type B's trust:
- Avoid debates
- Seek consensus
- Be patient and do not rush them

Best persuasion tactics to use with Type Bs:
- Be optimistic, friendly, and patient
- Recognize and appreciate them
- Give them a variety of options instead of this or that

Don'ts for Covertly Influencing Type B Manipulators:
- Don't be pessimistic or moody
- Don't dwell on the difficult tasks
- Don't shut yourself off from them

CHOOSE THE BEST LOCATION

Location can be an asset when you're looking to get a specific result from someone. Consider placing yourself in different environments when you're trying to change the dynamic of your relationship or you want to expand your influence. People can tie feelings and attitudes to specific spaces. For example, if intense discussions and arguments tend to occur in the kitchen, try moving those conversations outside.

If you regularly meet with your employees in your office to give constructive feedback, they may associate that space with discomfort or inferiority and become defensive. To break this pattern, consider using a conference room instead. Better yet, choose a neutral area that makes everyone more comfortable. If you take your employees for an offsite feedback meeting at a coffee shop where the uplifting atmosphere and caffeine can energize them, they might be more open to receiving constructive feedback. This shift in setting can help them take any criticisim less personally and make them more willing to engage in a positive manner.

When I was an interrogator at Guantanamo Bay in 2002, I met a detainee outside his cell block with the guards and my interpreter. All five us walked from the prison to the interrogation booths, going in and out of gates and past guard checks. During this fifteen-minute walk, I found the detainee to be very engaging and talkative. Once he was seated in my interrogation room, he became an entirely different person. His demeanor shifted from casual and talkative to closed off and quiet, but nothing had changed other than our physical location. Realizing this, I found a guard who had time to walk with us outside, and we eased back into conversation. The detainee associated an interrogation room with fear and the need to keep quiet. But under the Cuban sun, he readily answered my questions.

Get Them Moving

In the world of body language, there's a saying: "Move the body, move the mind." People feel more comfortable when they are in motion. Engaging in physical activity can suppress cortisol release and reduce stress.

Our thoughts directly influence our behavior. If we're thinking, "I'm worried, I'm angry, I can't take any more stress," then we will behave in a worried, angry, stressed manner. A physical boost from walking, stretching, or even standing can help shift our thoughts from our worries to the action at hand and calm us.

If you are in a conversation with someone who is getting emotional, take a walk with them to open up channels of communication.

Surprise Them

If you are engaging in a conversation with someone who has dark psychological traits and is used to dominating you, you can catch them off guard and disrupt their control by responding in an unexpected manner. This may instill fear or confusion in them, making them worry about what you might say or do next. They may start to fear losing control over you and the conversation. When a person is in this state, they are off balance, which means they may inadvertently reveal information or show compliance. Ask yourself these strategic questions to gain control: What can I say or do that they haven't observed before? What will make them second-guess their perception of dominance?

USE SILENCE TO YOUR ADVANTAGE

Depending on the culture, people feel uncomfortable with silence and usually want to jump into conversation to break it. In some cultures, like our own, just a few seconds of silence can cause a sense of unease. The more silence you allow, the more disconnected the other person will begin to feel. Let that panic build a little bit. They need to feel connected again, so wait it out and force them to break the silence. This covert technique works well to persuade someone to talk.

#6 CONTROL THE NARRATIVE

NOW THAT YOU'VE DISCOVERED COVERT WAYS TO INFLUENCE OTHERS by creating an environment that works in your favor (whether that means bringing the right energy, using the right body language, or choosing the right location to confront someone), it's time to develop tools for speaking strategically and forcefully to assert your power. In order to steer a conversation and remain in control, you should know how to use embedded commands and elicitation techniques. These techniques are so effective that spies use them (and have done so for centuries). I have used the strategies that follow to gather intelligence information from detainees without having to reveal what information I was seeking. You can utilize them when you want to confront someone and get honest answers so you can decide whether to trust them or not.

EMBEDDED COMMANDS

Embedded commands are a neuro-linguistic programming (NLP) technique for planting a thought beneath a person's conscious awareness. They're like subliminal messages that help you build rapport and accomplish what you want in a conversation. They can also be used to evoke key emotions or to point someone's answers in a specific direction. The ones I will share in this chapter will help you persuade someone to consider, imagine, decide, or share something.

An embedded command has three parts: the suggestion or command ("as you consider/imagine/decide/share"), the timing ("now," "as soon as"), and the effective outcome ("you will," "we can"). When delivering an embedded command, use all three parts to ensure its effectiveness.

To use embedded commands well, you must set out with a clear purpose. What message do you want to embed as a command? Do you want to influence someone to open up and share information with you? Do you want to persuade someone to like

NLP ORIGINS

Richard Bandler, a student at the University of California, Santa Cruz, listened to recordings of taped therapy sessions as part of his studies. He began to notice that certain words and sentence structures were more effective in getting the client to accept the therapist's suggestions. He invited John Grinder, a linguistics lecturer, to collaborate with him as he studied other therapists' recordings. They found that the embedded messages in ordinary speech weren't "heard" by the *conscious* mind, but they were detected by the *unconscious* mind. Together they produced a meta model, a model for gathering information and challenging a client's language and underlying thinking. They created neuro-linguistic programming (NLP) as an approach to communication, personal development, and psychotherapy.

USING EMBEDDED COMMANDS ETHICALLY

Do not use embedded commands with the intent to manipulate someone in a harmful way. When used for detecting deception, unconscious commands can add value for others, help them solve problems, and get them to say yes. Avoid being threatening or demanding, and use your own moral compass to guide you.

Former sex-cult leader Keith Raniere started Executive Success Programs (later rebranded under the name NXIVM) with Nancy Salzman, an NLP practitioner. She was a former psychiatric nurse and a trained hypnotist who used NLP in the darkest way possible: to get cult members to mentally submit to Raniere's communal rules. She would later serve three-and-a-half years in prison for her crimes.

you and promote you? Perhaps you want a colleague to introduce you to their friends to expand your network. Maybe you want the truth from someone close to you. All of these goals can be accomplished with embedded commands.

Convince Someone to Consider Your Perspective

If you want to encourage someone to **consider** your side of a story, you would make a statement that uses the command word, the timing, and the desired outcome.

- "As you **consider** my side of the story when I tell it to you, you will hear new information that may change your opinion." Then tell your side of the story.

- "**Consider** my side of the story now, and you will hear new information that may change your view." Then go on to explain your perspective.

- "As you **consider** my side of the story today, you will hear new information that may change your stance." Then you tell your side.

Convince Someone to Imagine a New Situation or Dynamic

If you want to encourage someone to **imagine** a better relationship that includes trust, you could say:

- "**Imagine** how we will feel down the road in our relationship when we trust each other."
- "**Imagine** what our relationship could be if we trusted each other."

Convince Someone to Decide to Be Honest

If you want to encourage someone to **decide** to be honest, you could say:

- "When you **decide** now to be honest, you will feel good sharing what you know with me."
- "**Deciding** today to be honest takes courage and will make you feel good for doing the right thing."

Convince Someone to Share Information

If you want to encourage someone to **share** information with you, you could say:

- "**Sharing** what you know now will help us both."
- "I can see you are now considering **sharing** what you know with me now because it will help us both."

THE GOLDEN RULES OF VERBAL COMMANDS

Some conversational scenarios are more challenging than others and present unique obstacles. Manipulators are out to confuse you, so of course they don't want to be confronted. They'd rather avoid all responsibility and accountability and play the victim so they can blame you for their behavior. This gives all the more reason to confront them using verbal commands in a tactical way:

Mask it

Buffer the embedded word so that it doesn't present as a command. You can use flattery or pretend to be naïve. For example:

- **Flattery:** "I admire how you never take things personally. I appreciate your openness to listening and **considering** my side of the story when I tell it. When I do give my side, you will hear new information that may change your opinion."

- **Naïveté:** "I have no idea how to approach certain topics. I feel like I have good intentions, but then I sound rude or nervous and sometimes upset people. My intention is always to be respectful. I'd like to share my thoughts and opinions with you and, as you **consider** what I say, you may change your perspective."

Emphasize it

While you can tuck the command word within your statement so that feels less like a command, it must be heard. To ensure that it's heard, you can increase the volume of your voice, pause before and after it, or deepen your tone. Never inflect your voice with an embedded command, or it will sound more like a question and lose its impact.

Time it

Include the timeframe somewhere in the command. Use words like "now," "immediately," or "this time." If this is done well, it will allow you to get to the truth, call someone out as the perpetrator, and hold them accountable for their behaviors.

ELICITATION TECHNIQUES

Elicitation is a method of getting information with strategic statements instead of asking questions. Questions can put a

WHO USES ELICITATION

Elicitation is used by military intelligence services worldwide, as well as law enforcement agencies and private-sector industries. In military intelligence, elicitation is an intelligence collection technique used in human intelligence (HUMINT) to gather information to answer intelligence requirements. Law enforcement personnel use elicitation to gather information from witnesses to help solve crimes, to collect information from a neighborhood during canvassing operations, or to coax a suspect into confession.

In the private sector, elicitation is also used as a business intelligence tool for making better-informed decisions to gain a competitive advantage in their industry. For example, marketers may want to acquire information on future market forecasts, health professionals may want to find out what is really troubling patients, C-suite executives may want to obtain information on their competition, trade-show attendees may want to develop actionable business leads rather than a pocket full of business cards, and business owners want to hire a trusted team. The list of uses goes on.

subject on guard, especially when they come across as intrusive. The subject may feel that you are too curious about who they are and what they know. They might feel as though they are being interrogated. Questions also draw attention to the type of information you are trying to collect and can blow your cover. Elicitation allows us to relax the target and gain trust from the person all while concealing our objective and intent. What comes across as a mundane conversation is actually a carefully planned one. If you are good at elicitation, your statement provokes a response from your subject (either agreement, disagreement, or information) of their own free will.

Why Does Elicitation Work So Well?

Elicitation works so well because it takes its cues from human psychology and human nature. It rests on the proven assumptions that:

- People want to be polite, honest, and trustworthy, and they want to believe that others are polite, honest, and trustworthy, too.
- People do not like to be wrong. They want to prove they are right and that they're more knowledgeable than others.
- People like to hear themselves talk, educate others, correct others, and show off what they know because it makes them feel intelligent.
- People like to complain, whether individually or, preferably, as part of a group.
- People seek recognition and praise and they want to feel appreciated and thanked.
- People have a hard time keeping secrets and they have a tendency to gossip.
- People are less discreet when they are emotional.

- People tend to underestimate the value of the information they have and how that information could be used against them.

- People tend to make decisions based on emotion rather than reason.

- People take pride in what they know, and will try to convert people to their opinion.

When Is Elicitation a Valuable Tool?

Anywhere, anytime, and with anyone, but more specifically:

- When you want to find out personal information, like opinions, industry knowledge, or other sensitive information and it would be unwise or unacceptable to ask.

- When you don't want to scare off or offend your target by asking too many questions and making them feel interrogated.

- When you are unsure who has the information you need, or who has the placement for access to the information you need.

- When you don't know what you don't know. Elicitation is a great way to determine if the information someone has is valuable and worth investing your time in.

- When you need to get a deeper understanding of information that has been only partly released to the public or when you need an unbiased view of that information.

- When you want to put someone at ease and get more of their time. If you have an unassuming conversation that appears to be casual in nature to your subject, they are more likely to give you more of their time instead of shutting down from discomfort.

- When you need to gain information that, if you named it, people would not be willing to share. For example, maybe you need to know what the market is forecasting, what your competition is doing, or what threats exist in your area.

- When you need to help others. Sometimes people are too embarrassed or scared to tell you how they really feel or what they really know. A good example of this is when patients feel too ashamed or embarrassed to discuss health problems with health professionals, or when a suspect or witness is too scared to share information or point out the perpetrator for fear of retaliation.

The Best Elicitation Techniques

Here are eight highly effective elicitation techniques to help you get crucial information from someone without their knowing.

1. Help Me: Helping others makes people feel good about themselves. Rarely will you encounter someone who will not help you. This technique exploits that aspect of human psychology. You will most likely use this technique in conjunction with others, such as flattery, naïveté, and showing interest.

- "I bet you have some sound advice that could help me, with your background and expertise."
- "I would love some help; I've never done this before."
- "I'm new to this area, so I will gladly take anyone's help!"
- "I haven't dated in a while, so you may have to help me feel comfortable."
- "Help me understand why you are covering up for your friends."
- "Help me make sense of this situation."
- "I'm not a mind reader. Help me understand your point of view so that I can better understand your needs."

2. Naïveté: Playing naïve encourages a knowledgeable (or egotistical) individual to educate you. This technique requires you to suspend your ego and portray yourself as naïve, ignorant, or unaware of something. Sometimes you actually will be unaware! If your target enjoys talking about themselves and their work, and considers themselves to be an expert in something, this technique will be highly effective. If you use naïveté on targets who are ruled by their ego, they will not have the willpower to keep secrets or sensitive information. Usually, your target will associate positive emotions with you when you use this strategy and will like you more. Some targets, however, may respond negatively to this technique. This includes individuals who only want to be around smart, knowledgeable, and accomplished people. The trick is to be naïve to a degree but not so naïve that you turn your target away.

Let's say you just started dating a new guy, and you want to know whether he is financially stable and savvy in his financial decisions, or if he is in credit card debt and never pays his bills on time. You could say, "I'm a bit naïve when it comes to managing finances. I always seem to make poor financial decisions." If he says, "Oh, me too. Don't feel bad," you may not want that second date after all.

3. The One-Up Bait: Think of this technique as the *I bet you can't beat/top this!* strategy. You make a statement that acts as bait to get your target to share something while trying to one-up you. This technique works well on targets with bigger egos who feel compelled to prove that they're smarter. Use this technique with caution for two reasons. First, it will not be effective if you use it on a more modest person. Second, if you use it on a target who has a bigger ego, they may start to embellish what they say, which only gets you false, over-the-top information. You do not want to inadvertently push the target into giving you false information. Another version of the one-up bait is the "reflective" statement when you share information about someone else instead of yourself. This way, you can get out of having to back up what you said with more details (because you don't have all the details). When using this technique, your target will typically respond with something such as, "Oh yeah, well, I know. . . ," "Ah well, I know. . . ," "Hmmm, it only took me. . . ," or "That's nothing. I can. . ."

Let's say you think your husband's friend and colleague, Evan, is out to undermine him and take his position. You are out to dinner with your husband Tom, Evan, and his wife. You can say, "Evan, I bet you heard that the C-suite is impressed with what Tom has been doing in his new position." Evan might take the bait and say, "Yeah, I heard. Let's see how they feel about him after the honeymoon stage. It's easy to impress people in the first month. It's longevity they look for." Or maybe he'll alleviate your suspicions and say, "They are. There is no better person for that position. Good job, Tom!"

4. Quid Pro Quo: The Latin term "quid pro quo," or "this for that," means that if I give you something, you give me something. The simplest form of quid pro quo occurs when we meet someone new: We give them our name, and they give us their name in return. You might even notice that if you give both your first and last name they'll reply with their first and last name.

Think about the information you want and offer something similar in order to get it. For example, if you want to find out what your target's favorite sport or hobby is, you could say, "I like skiing," and hope that your target reciprocates with their favorite pastime. It's best to create a story around your provocative quid pro quo statement to encourage a smooth transition and credibility. For example, instead of just awkwardly stating your hobby out of nowhere, say, "I'm thankful summer is finally here. I've been itching to get back on the water. There are a few things in life I can't live without, and fishing is one of them!"

When you use quid pro quo, some targets will try to one-up you with an experience, education, employment, embarrassing moment, and so on. Let them! In a sense, this is using the One-Up Bait and Quid Pro Quo together. For example, "I'll tell you about a time when I...," "When I was young I didn't always do the right thing. I remember one time...," "We're all human, and even I make mistakes. Wait until you hear this one... "

This one can also be used reflectively with someone else's thoughts or experiences as the bait. For example, instead of saying, "I heard that to work at the Pentagon, you need a top-secret clearance," you would say, "A friend of mine said that if you want to work at the Pentagon, you need top-secret clearance."

5. Word Repetition: Repeating what someone has said can enhance interpersonal involvement in a conversation and the overall comprehension of a conversation. It can persuade others to share information and disclose more details about a particular topic. All you have to do is actively listen to what your target says and repeat a word or phrase to encourage them to keep talking. This is also called parroting. It's an easy way to coax a person to keep expanding on a topic. There are pros and cons to using word repetition, however.

- Pros: Repeating the same word(s) your target uses at the end of a conversation shows that you are paying attention to what they are saying. It also encourages the target to say more about that word or topic.

- Cons: This technique can backfire because you may come across as listening too intently and arouse your target's suspicion. It can also seem contrived or silly if overused. Use this technique sparingly or you will draw attention to yourself and cause mistrust.

6. Take an Opposing Stand: To use this technique, there has to be a dichotomy, or two opposing sides, to an issue or belief. Begin by clearly taking one side, preferably the opposite side of your target, in order to encourage them to open up as they try to convince you to see their side. It helps to have a sense of where your target stands before using this strategy. Your hope is that they'll become emotional and indiscreet with the information they share because they have taken on persuading you as a personal conquest.

This is an effective technique to draw out sensitive or secret information from others. Be careful, however, because you could unintentionally upset your target or cause them to walk away if they feel frustrated or believe that they cannot win this battle of persuasion. If taken too far, this technique could turn into an unhealthy debate. Make sure you control your emotions, remain respectful, and listen to what your target is saying. Do not take what your target says personally or your healthy debate may turn into an argument. Consider your target's personality preference before using this technique, as it can be too confrontational for some. Others may enjoy debating so much they push you into an argument. Some examples of common dichotomies you can

REAL-LIFE ELICITATION: WORD REPETITION TO CATCH A MURDERER

Drew Peterson, the convicted murderer, was interviewed by Larry King in 2008, after his fourth wife went mysteriously missing but before he'd been convicted of his third wife's murder. When discussing how he treated his wife, he said, "I'm a police officer. I don't work for the phone company or the power company, and as a police officer we don't have the same ability to [do] things as the common person. If I get involved in a domestic situation where I'm physical with a wife, I'll lose my job and I would never even care to even come close to risking that."

If you were to use word repetition on Peterson to elicit information, you might say, "So you would lose your job if you were physical with a wife," or "So you wouldn't risk losing your job by being physical with your wife," or "So a common person has the ability to be physical with a wife." Then you'd stop and wait. The only way that this technique works is if you refrain from speaking after repeating back what they said. This keeps them talking and offering enough detail to expose their lies.

exploit are politics, religion, technology, pro-life/pro-choice, gun laws, and health care.

7. Complain: This technique takes advantage of your target's desire to explain, commiserate, or brag about a topic of your choice. You may have heard the saying "Misery loves company," which means people often enjoy complaining together. If you and your target complain about the same issue, it can create a sense of connection and validate their feelings. When you get someone to start complaining, you might encourage them to release their emotions and let their guard down enough to share information.

You might say something like, "It's hard to believe that this country doesn't have a better health care system," "Life is unfair," "You can't trust anyone on a dating app these days; their photos are AI generated and ChatGPT writes their profiles for them," or "You shouldn't have listened to them; they don't know anything."

Warning: If your target becomes too upset, it could damage your rapport and shut down the conversation. If they associate negative emotions with you, it may hinder future interactions. If this happens, try to redirect the conversation to a different topic and encourage them to mirror your calm demeanor until they relax.

Exploiting the desire to complain can strengthen your target's ego. When people complain, they typically prefer to take the stance that they know better than you. Allowing your target to boost their ego can have both advantages and disadvantages:

- **Advantages:** If you let the target build their self-esteem, they may feel compelled to educate or teach you, thus providing you with valuable information.

- **Disadvantages:** If you allow the target to feel superior, they may lose interest in teaching you or feel that you aren't worth their time.

8. Provide False Information: This technique is, in my opinion, the easiest to use and the most effective. It's designed to get the target to prove to you that you are wrong and they are right. You might provide false information for them to disprove and wait for them to educate you or correct you. They're bound to give up information in the process. Keep in mind that your target may be introverted and may need time to process the information you give them before responding, so be patient.

Here are some examples for using this technique. You might say, "I read somewhere that (insert false information)," "That's not what I heard. I heard that (insert false information)," or "We found out that (insert false information)."

Using Elicitation When Someone Shuts Down

To keep the conversation going when your colleague or love interest gives you a soft denial like, "I don't want to talk about it," try these elicitation techniques to get more information:

SPIES AND ELICITATION

Elicitation is the primary method used by spy recruiters who set out to spot, assess, bump, and recruit new spies. They excel at identifying potential spies by spotting them first (SPOT). Once identified, recruiters study the patterns of these individuals and gather extensive information about them (ASSESS).

After this assessment, recruiters often orchestrate a "chance" encounter (BUMP). Although it appears to be coincidental, it is actually carefully planned. During this seemingly ordinary conversation, recruiters aim to establish rapport and gauge whether the target might be interested in spying for their country. If they are, the relationship is established between the spy and their handler (RECRUIT).

Spy recruiters employ covert conversational techniques to broach the subject of espionage, because approaching a foreign national directly and asking if they would like to spy on their own country could get you arrested and cause grave international repercussions.

Use a Combination of Showing Interest, Embedded Command, and Assigning a Positive Trait: "I want you to feel comfortable. You and I can be open with each other. I know that you aren't afraid to tell me what's on your mind."

Use "Help Me": "I want you to feel comfortable and safe. I need your help in understanding how to do that so we can be open with each other about anything."

Use Quid Pro Quo: "I don't like talking about X either, but I will for us."

Express Disbelief: "We are great communicators. I can't believe we can't feel comfortable enough with each other to talk about this."

Use Flattery: "You are the strong one when it comes to having difficult conversations. I will follow your lead. I am open and appreciate hearing anything you feel comfortable telling me."

Make an Indirect Reference: You can approach a delicate or sensitive topic indirectly at first to ease your way into the conversation, especially if the other person is expressing reluctance. For example, if they say something like, "I don't know if I feel comfortable answering those questions or discussing that topic," you can encourage them to communicate by opening up with other topics and later segue into the issue. For example, you can say, "I respect that. Help me understand how I can make you feel comfortable," or "I value that. Let's talk about something I know you will be comfortable with."

Take your time and be patient. That is sometimes the most challenging part of guiding a conversation. If you rush it, you will feel anxious and the other person may sense your insecurity and nervousness and stop trusting you. We tend to immediately trust confident people, so it is imperative that you remain calm and confident. When you feel relaxed and sure of yourself, the person you are communicating with will feel that way too. This phenomenon is referred to as emotional contagion or mirror neurons.

Using Elicitation When Someone Refuses to Talk

To keep the conversation going when your colleague or love interest gives you a firm refusal like, "I'm not going to answer that," try these tactics to get more information:

Use Word Repetition: Address their refusal to answer instead of ignoring it. Why? Because ignoring it makes it seem like you're not listening to them. Asking the same question again, even if it's later on, can come across as sneaky and can jeopardize your relationship. Instead, when they say, "I don't want to get into that now; now is not a good time for me," you can repeat the phrase, "So now is not a good time."

They may explain why it's not a good time or they may shut down and say "Yeah." If they shut down, try one more time. Say something slightly more defined such as, "Then it's not a good time right now." Only use word repetition twice. Any more and you will sound suspicious and inauthentic.

Acknowledge Their Refusal and Make a Provocative Statement: Remember, provocative statements will encourage the other person to willingly, albeit unwittingly, share information. When they do share that information (as most people are likely to do), they don't feel that you were being pushy, because you never asked a question. They are providing information of their own free will. Here are some provocative statements to encourage openness and honesty when someone refuses to talk:

- "I hear you. My intention is *not* to make you feel uncomfortable; it is to comfort you with an *open* and *honest* conversation free of any judgment." (**Naïveté**)
- "I didn't realize that this topic would cause you concern or make you uncomfortable." Pause and wait for their response (**Naïveté** elicitation technique).
- "I'm listening. Help me see it from your point of view." (**"Help Me"** elicitation technique).

If you know how to handle their refusal to admit to their "crimes," you'll get the results you want and learn the truth behind the dark psychology.

GETTING A NARCISSIST TO TALK

If you are dealing with a person who has narcissistic tendencies, it may be impossible to build rapport with them, because they don't have a lot of empathy. Instead, the goal is to focus on concrete facts and keep feelings and emotions out of the conversation. Instead of sharing information about yourself or trying to establish an emotional connection, the key is to flatter them and play to their ego while remaining confident and credible. Go too big and they'll see right through you. Try some of the strategic phrasings below to get them to talk, reveal, and comply:

- "I don't want to impose on your time, but with your expertise in this matter, I know what you have to say will make a significant impact."
- "I'm seeking your help, so I'm on your timeline. I really would appreciate hearing your point of view."

- "I've been in this business for years, so I've learned to value other people's time, especially people in your position/with your experience."

- "I like the way you think/handled that/command respect. I bet that comes naturally for a person in your position."

- "You sound like you're a natural leader. I would be eager to hear your advice for/on ..."

- "Your reputation precedes you, which is probably why (name of person/company) told me to contact you personally." Note: Reputation is critical for them, which means

---

CONVERSATION COMMAND TIPS

Remember these steps to keep your thoughts organized as you work to gain control of a challenging conversation:

1. Focus on and remember the exact words they use in their responses. It will help you be able to parrot them, so listen carefully.

2. Address their statements directly, especially if they sound suspicious or don't ring true to you. Either ask an interrogative question or use an elicitation technique for further clarification.

3. Be objective in how you call them out on any inappropriate or inexcusable behavior. Do not name-call, judge, or label.

4. Make them back up their statements. Ask them for evidence or examples. If they can't provide them, then you need to tell them what they say has no weight or validity. They may be stating how they feel, but it's not necessarily the truth.

5. Don't show any signs of doubting yourself. Be patient. Exude confidence, even if it's an act.

they won't do anything to damage it. If they believe that something will damage their reputation, they can be persuaded to behave differently.

- "It's hard for me to empathize with people who are lazy/don't apply themselves/don't want to listen when help is offered." Note: Here you are taking their perspective and validating them.

Deescalating Tactics for Personal Safety

When a dispute arises, the last thing you want to do is say something that will escalate disruptive or abusive behavior. To protect yourself from this, try these deescalating tactics.

1. Step outside the conflict to see another perspective.

Try to take an observer's point of view of the conversation and the context behind it. This may mean asking the other person why they said what they did. Try to remove your emotions and look past your own view. Avoid assigning blame or claiming to be right. Just listen. This way they can't blame you for their disruptive or abusive behavior.

Try to think in terms of a win-win situation. A win-win situation requires an alternative conclusion to arguing that can benefit you both. Try to converse like you are on the same team. Be cooperative and try to find solutions together. You may not succeed in this if you are dealing with a person who has dark psychological traits, but you can try. Your focus is to deescalate a potential argument and create a safe environment for yourself so that you can remove yourself from the situation or physical location without harm.

REAL-LIFE CASE STUDY: CONTROLLING THE NARRATIVE

I will never forget a litigant I interviewed while working as an interrogation expert on *Couples Court with the Cutlers*. This guy had such disdain for me that I had to cleverly trick him into telling the truth. His girlfriend brought him on the show after accusing him of cheating on her with his ex-girlfriend (with whom he had a child). She claimed that he left the house every morning at 4:00 a.m. and returned at 6:00 a.m. to make breakfast and get their kids on the bus. She alleged that he was sleeping with his ex during those hours.

He denied the accusation, insisting that he was actually going to the park at that time to work out, and then heading to the mosque to pray at 5:00 a.m. When we discovered that the mosque didn't even open until 9:00 a.m., I knew he was lying and was determined to find out the truth.

When I challenged his account on the basis of the mosque being closed, he claimed that he knew the Imam well and was allowed into the mosque even when it was officially closed. It

Wrong move:

You speak up, act accusatory, and become aggressive. This could upset them and cause them to retaliate. Your safety and well-being is more important than your pride. Remember that.

Right move:

Speak up with confidence, kindness, and empathy. Say what you need to say while being respectful and empathetic in order to keep the other person's emotions and temper at bay. If you

was evident to me that he was being deceptive. His incongruent shoulder shrugs and expression said it all. He was a bad liar.

Given that he disliked me and exhibited narcissistic behavior, like looking down his nose at me, leaking disgust in his facial expression, and rolling his eyes, I decided not to try to win him over but rather to persuade him to tell the truth by commanding the narrative. I appealed to his value system and his attachment to his reputation with the statement, "As a Muslim male, you are responsible for the women in your life. You have to take care of them." He agreed. I continued by saying, "It's your responsibility to take care of your ex and the child you're raising child with her. If you didn't, then you would be considered a coward—not a man in your faith."

This made him angry. He straightened up, scowled at me, and replied, "Yeah, I do [need to take care of my ex and our child]. That's why I go over there every morning!"

I smiled and thanked him. He tried to retract his words, but it was too late. He went on to fail his polygraph test. He was indeed cheating on this woman with his ex-girlfriend.

put in the work to be empathetic and respectful, and they continue to lie, deny, or refuse to talk, you can still safely end the conversation and make a decision later about whether you want to continue your relationship with this individual.

2. Address one issue at a time. Don't pile on others.

When we argue, we tend to bring up other topics that have nothing to do with the problem at hand. We may even bring up events that happened years ago. Doing this just adds fuel to the fire. The conflict will multiply and veer into less-relevant topics. To control a conversation, stay on track and keep the other person on track.

3. Listen objectively, without your internal voice.

It's difficult to divide our attention between listening and thinking about what we want to say. Usually, one or the other falls off.

To listen and retain accurate information from someone, we must quiet our internal voice. When your mind wanders off from listening to someone, bring your attention back to what that person is saying.

When people feel as though you are listening to them, they think that what they are saying has importance. That alone can quickly deescalate a conflict.

4. Own your part and your actions; take responsibility.

Step up to the plate. If you are involved in a conflict, you may be partly responsible. Think about what you have said or done, or have not said or done, that contributed to the conflict. Be objective. Step outside yourself and remove your emotions. Analyze your actions and reactions.

5. Focus on what you can control—not what you can't.

You can control conflict. Instead of focusing on the other person's reactions, concentrate on your own. Instead of worrying about the other person's emotions, control your emotions. Instead of being concerned about the other person's ego, focus on your ego. You will find that the more you focus on the things you can influence, the more influence you will have. Instead of trying to persuade someone to take your point of view, let it go and know that they will think what they want. You may have to agree to disagree.

#7 STEP INTO YOUR POWER, #8 TURN THE TABLES, AND #9 SET BOUNDARIES

SHARED POWER AND DECISIONS ARE A NORMAL PART OF EVERY RELATIONSHIP. In a romantic partnership, it's acceptable to compromise on things like the type of car you buy, the tile you choose for a bathroom remodel, or who will take care of the litter box. Sacrificing your core values or your dignity should never be acceptable. If you are in a work, romantic, or family relationship with someone who undermines your self-worth, happiness, or safety through dark psychology, it's time to respect yourself enough to rise up and take back your life. Persistent ridicule, criticism, biting sarcasm, and backhanded compliments (negging) are the weapons someone can use to take away your power through dark psychology.

SIGNS THAT YOU NEED TO RECLAIM YOUR POWER

If you're still wondering if you're overthinking a situation or being dramatic, it helps to do a status check on your power in a relationship. In the case of a partner controlling you, it's because they want to feel bigger.

Here are some signs that you need to take your power back:

- They tell you what to wear, how to look, and what to say. For example, a romantic partner might not allow you to wear makeup or sexy clothes because you will look too good.
- They control your spending.
- They ask you to quit your job because you rank higher than them at work or make more money.
- Their definition of quality time is doing what they like to do.
- They try to limit your social interaction or control who you're friends with.
- They have sex on their terms only. They aim to satisfy themselves when it comes to sex, with little regard for your pleasure and satisfaction, or they withhold sex as a bargaining chip to get you to do what they want.
- They lie to you about infidelity or finances, or betray you in other big ways.
- They threaten or abuse you verbally or physically, have rage issues, or exhibit other dangerous and toxic traits.

OVERCOMING DEEP FEARS AND FINDING YOUR CONFIDENCE

Joanna Kleinman, a certified psychotherapist and the author of *Dethroning Your Inner Critic*, created a method to help people overcome their fears and self-limiting beliefs by turning them into a source of power that can instead help them achieve personal growth, happiness, and confidence. It takes deep internal thought work, something we can only do for ourselves.

According to Kleinman, our primal fears can inhibit us from stepping into our own power, whether that means applying for a more challenging job, entering into a new relationship after ending a toxic one, or speaking up and telling your coworker or best friend that they are treating you unfairly. Stepping into your power is living a life that is aligned to your true self—your morals, ethics, and beliefs— and reaching your full potential on your terms.

Our primal fears can prevent us from reaching our potential. These fears, whether caused by nature or nurture, are housed in our primitive brain and emotional center, the limbic brain. They influence our choices in ways we may not even realize. Let's say that you experience a setback or failure in your career after taking on the responsibility of a new project. You may feel as though your confidence and credibility have been stripped away. As a result, you may feel unimportant and insecure. Your primitive brain (emotional center) logs that feeling, so anytime a new opportunity arises at work, you may say to yourself, *I never want to experience that failure again because it made me feel insecure and unsafe, so I will avoid taking on new responsibilities.* Your career may suffer as a result. You may never reach your goals and aspirations because your primal fear is steering your career decisions.

Kleinman believes that we can challenge those limiting assumptions and push past them to regain new confidence. When we make a conscious decision to venture outside of our comfort zone and embrace failure as a learning experience instead of a setback, we can regain control over our life decisions. We may have to reassure ourselves and remind ourselves to embrace these failures. We may have to tell ourselves that we will be OK even if, for example, we bomb the test or get fired, or if our partner leaves us. Here's how someone can move from a place of doubt and disempowerment to one of confidence and control:

Tell Your Story

The first step in getting distance from the effects of gaslighting, guilt-tripping, and shaming is to regain confidence in your own narrative and your own perspective.

- **Tell others about the manipulation:** Nothing is more freeing than talking about your experience with those you trust. Just the act of telling your story can be healing and can inspire new realizations.
- **Share it with those who can help:** There may be some value that your story can offer others or courage it can inspire in those with similar circumstances.

Challenge and Reject Negative Labels

If there is dark psychology at play in your relationship, you may have been called words like "selfish," "weak," and "ungrateful" to make you doubt yourself. Casting off these labels means testing and challenging their objective validity. You'll discover that they're not accurate assessments but collateral damage caused by a master manipulator.

Ask Yourself Questions:

- *Is this label based on reality or their distorted perspective?*
- *What evidence supports or contradicts this label?*

Flip Negative Labels to Their Positive Truths

- Replace the idea of yourself as **selfish** with *I'm setting healthy boundaries and I deserve that. I deserve to be respected.*

- Replace the idea of yourself as **weak** with *I'm working through challenges and growing stronger.*

- Instead of thinking, **"I'm not good enough"**, remind yourself that someone wanted you to feel worthless in order to control you. Instead of believing that you always say the wrong thing, remind yourself that someone made you feel like everything you said was wrong so that you wouldn't speak out against them.

Reconnect with Your Authentic Self

Manipulation can hide us from ourselves; journaling can get us back in touch with ourselves. To reclaim your power, find space to be alone so that you can write with honesty about what's essential, powerful, and true about yourself. If writing isn't your thing, you can just sit with your thoughts or take a walk as you:

- **Reflect on your strengths:** Write down qualities you admire about yourself, such as kindness, resilience, or creativity. These are traits that manipulation may have overshadowed but that still exist within you.

- **Revisit your values:** Identify what matters most to you—maybe it's honesty, compassion, or independence—and use these values to guide your decisions moving forward.

- **Practice self-compassion:** Forgive yourself for any perceived mistakes during the manipulation. Remember, you were doing the best you could under difficult circumstances.

Only you know the person you've always been and always will be. Don't let your manipulator tell you who you are.

Rebuild Confidence Through Action

Confidence isn't just a mindset—it's driven by your actions. The more actions you take for yourself to regain peace and control, the more ready you'll feel to stand tall against manipulation.

- **Set small, achievable goals:** Start with something manageable, like taking a class, exercising regularly, or reaching out to a supportive friend. Accomplishing goals reminds you that you have agency.

- **Celebrate wins:** Acknowledge every victory, no matter how small. If the controlling person in your life labels you as lazy or worthless, but this time you challenged them on it, recognize how much courage that took.

- **Seek empowering experiences:** Engage in activities that make you feel inspired and capable, like learning martial arts, leading a volunteer group, or hiking a mountain.

When you turn your passive role into an active one, you'll notice how it puts you in the driver's seat (or at least assures you that you'll be back there soon).

Reframe Feelings of Insecurity

Insecurity can linger even after you've removed the degrading person from your life, but you can actually use it to build your confidence. Rebrand insecurity as sign of progress and you can turn it from a limitation into a motivator.

- **View insecurity as evidence of your growth:** Feeling insecure doesn't mean you're weak—it means you're doing something uncomfortable and wrestling with that challenge. For example, you might feel insecure when you try to reconnect with the friends you have cut out of your life as a result of a bad relationship. The important thing is not that you're insecure but that you're putting yourself out there.

- **Practice positive self-talk:** Replace thoughts like *I can't do this* with *I'm learning and improving every day.*
- **Draw from past resilience:** Reflect on times you overcame challenges before. If you made it through before, you can do it again.

Surround Yourself with Supportive People

A key to stepping into your power is fostering relationships with people who uplift and validate you.

- **Seek out positive influences:** Spend time with friends, family, or mentors who genuinely care about your well-being and celebrate your growth.
- **Distance yourself from negative influences:** Reduce or eliminate contact with anyone who continues to manipulate, belittle, or undermine you.
- **Join support groups or communities:** Connecting with others who have overcome similar situations can provide inspiration and encouragement.

Cultivate a Growth Mindset

Rather than viewing the experience of manipulation as a failure, reframe it as an opportunity to grow.

- **Learn from the experience:** Ask yourself:
  - *What did this teach me about my boundaries?*
  - *How can I use this experience to strengthen myself?*

Seek Professional Help if Needed

Dark psychology can leave deep scars, so you may need to seek help to heal fully. Professional support can accelerate your journey to reclaiming your self-confidence.

Step into Your Power (S.I.Y.P.)

Once you reject the toxic elements of your manipulative relationship, confidence will naturally follow over time.

REAL-LIFE EXAMPLE: ESCAPING A CULT

Bethany Joy Lenz played Haley Scott on "One Tree Hill," a very popular TV show in the early 2000s. She became a follower of Michael Galeotti, a Christian pastor who founded Wild Branch Ministries, an organization that she describes now as a Christian cult. She ended up marrying Galeotti's son, Michael. According to Lenz, her husband and his family controlled her, her career, and her finances. Worse than that, she claims that Michael physically abused her. She alienated herself from her family and didn't speak to her father or brother for years.

Cult leaders brainwash their subjects into compliance with their beliefs. It is a way to exercise abusive control over others. They also seek to isolate subjects from their former lives by persuading them to live with one another in a commune-like setting. The leader of the cult usually insists that all followers abide by strict regiment around sleeping, eating, working, and relationships. They must be completely obedient. A reward and punishment system is usually put in place

- **Affirm your strength daily:** Use affirmations like:
  - *I am in control of my life.*
  - *I am worthy of respect and love.*
  - *I release the hold others have had on me and embrace my true power.*

- **Be the person you want to be:** Define yourself on your terms, not someone else's. Decide where you want to go next with your life and take steps to see that vision through.

---

to enforce the rules. Some cult leaders have been known to physically or emotionally torture unwilling or resistant followers using drugs, sleep deprivation, and other means. It's no surprise that many cult leaders have a God complex: They view themselves as higher beings, even to the extent of believing they are Gods.

In 2012, Lenz divorced Galeotti and left the church. By this point, she reported, the cult had taken $2 million from her and left her broke. She had lost her self-worth and her net worth as a result of this toxic relationship. She battled embarrassment and shame, exposing her story and writing about it in her memoir, *Dinner for Vampires*. In a *Vanity Fair* article titled "I Was in a Cult for 10 Years," she offers the following insight: "The more you talk about it, the less the shame has power over you. Shame is so detrimental. It keeps you isolated." This is undoubtedly true, and very clearly the words of someone who has emerged from the trap of dark psychology and is learning to reclaim her power. Once you recognize the truth—that you've been the victim of dark psychology—and accept that you can't change the past, you have to work on finding the courage to talk about your experience so you can help others.

TRUE CRIME CASE STUDY: NXIVM

Keith Raniere is a chilling example of a dark psychology expert and cult leader. Raniere, the cofounder and leader of the NXIVM cult, is now in prison on charges of attempted sex trafficking, forced labor conspiracy, wire fraud conspiracy, and racketeering.

He gathered quite a following and successfully recruited hundreds of men and women, even famous Hollywood actresses, business executives, and Harvard grads, to join his multilevel marketing scheme branded as a self-help program. He was very persuasive and convinced his followers to think and act how he wanted them to, even if it went against their own moral code. One subgroup of NXIVM was a secret sorority called DOS (a Latin acronym meaning "Lord/Master of the Obedient Female Companions"). The women were assigned the role of slaves and performed sexual acts on, Raniere their master. They were even persuaded to brand their pelvic area with Raniere's initials using a hot cauterizing pen.

Raniere garnered their admiration and trust. He kept them reliant on him because he isolated them from the outside world. They were cut off from speaking to friends and family members on the outside, and he exerted coercive control over them. Eventually, some members started to leave NXIVM because of their concerns about Raniere's godlike opinion of himself (he had everyone call him Vanguard, which came from a video game he played) and alleged acts of sexual manipulation with some of the women in the organization. In 2020, these reports of abuse led to his arrest. Raniere currently resides in the United States penitentiary in Tucson, where he's serving a 120-year sentence.

TURNING THE TABLES

Shifting the power dynamic on a manipulative person requires strategy, emotional control, and an ability to disrupt their expectations. Using the element of surprise effectively can turn the tables in your favor. Here's how to do it:

1. **Identify their patterns:** Manipulative people often follow predictable tactics, such as guilt-tripping about the same things (maybe you go out with your friends too much, or didn't attend to their needs in the way they wanted you to), gaslighting along the same narrative (that text you think is shady probably is), or exploiting your vulnerabilities in a predictable way (maybe they question your food choice at a restaurant in front of friends because they know it will strike deep). Identify the person's common strategies so you can anticipate their moves and potentially head them off in a way that reduces their power.

2. **Stay calm and collected:** manipulators rely on emotional reactions. If you remain composed, you deny them the leverage they seek. If you can detach emotionally from their provocations, you can get the upper hand.

3. **Disrupt their script:** Respond in unexpected ways to break their rhythm. For example: If they try to guilt-trip you, acknowledge their point without taking responsibility for it: "I see why you feel that way, but I disagree." If they exaggerate or lie, ask direct, clarifying questions that expose inconsistencies. Let's say your boss tries to guilt you into staying late by saying, "I thought you were a team player, but I guess I was wrong." Instead of reacting defensively, you could calmly reply, "I hear you and I disagree. I am a

strong team player. Why do you think this particular task should fall on me?" This unexpected response forces them to explain themselves and challenges their attempt to manipulate you.

4. Use silence as a weapon: Silence can be unnerving for someone used to controlling conversations. It forces them to fill the void, often exposing their motives. Instead of rushing to respond to a question from them, pause deliberately and let them overplay their hand.

5. Flip the focus back on them: Manipulators try to avoid accountability. Shift the focus to them with pointed questions:

- "Why do you think that's my responsibility?"
- "What are you hoping to achieve by saying that?"

6. Act out of character: To reverse the power balance in a toxic relationship, your best strategy is to do and say the unexpected. If they expect you to act defensively, for example, respond with humor or indifference. When a manipulator can't anticipate your next move, it becomes much more difficult for them to control you.

7. Take something away: Something is driving the manipulator's toxic behavior. Consider what it is they want and what matters most to them. Once you do, determine how to take it away covertly, without their realizing. If you do it right, they will be left baffled by the new terms of your relationship and unsettled by your newfound confidence.

Real-Life Profile: An Email to My Stalker

Long ago, I had a stalker, and the only thing that helped me get rid of him was to turn the tables and confront him (safely) over

KNOW WHAT THEY VALUE MOST

Things that matter most to those who use dark psychology include any or all the following:
- How people perceive them
- Money
- Status
- Relationships
- Having control over you

If you can figure out a way to pull any of these "rugs" out from under them, you can lessen their power.

email. We worked for the same agency in the D.C. area, and I started to notice that he was always in the cafeteria and the gym when I was there. He had learned my schedule and would show up to try to talk to me. I was always polite, but I made it clear in my words and behavior that I was not interested in getting to know him better or date him.

One day, he sent me an email asking what RKOLOGY meant. Those were the letters on my license plate. At that point I became nervous. He obviously knew my car. What else did he know about me, and was he watching me when I wasn't aware? A week later, I was pulling into a parking space at my apartment complex, and there he was. He pulled up beside me and acted like it was a coincidence that he had run into me in my underground parking garage. I told him that I didn't have time to talk and ran to the elevator.

Based on advice from my colleagues and my supervisor, I replied to his license plate email with the following message:

You made me very uncomfortable showing up at my apartment complex yesterday when you don't live there. Please do not do that again. I am not interested in any relationship with you. If you continue to follow me, I will have to take this to the CO [Commanding Officer]. Thank you.

Fortunately, he disappeared. I was worried about retaliation for some time afterward, so I made sure I never went anywhere alone. The email made it clear that if he retaliated or continued to stalk me, there would be grave consequences for him and his future. I caught him by surprise, took charge, and did what I could to take control of the situation. If this hadn't worked, I could have tried some of the other tactics that work against dark psychology. I might have tried to control the narrative or covertly influence him, but in the case of this person, stepping into my power and confronting him with confidence worked.

SETTING BOUNDARIES TO KEEP DARK PSYCHOLOGY AT BAY

Manipulative individuals often exploit emotional vulnerabilities, and without firm boundaries, it's all too easy to get pulled into their web. You may care deeply for someone, but if they engage in unacceptable behaviors, then you can either suffer their

THE DANGERS OF CALLING OUT A MANIPULATOR

Confront with caution. A person with dark psychological tendencies may retaliate against you if you call them out. You need a support network, and you need to make sure your support group knows everything going on and your whereabouts at all times. Never be unreachable. Never go anywhere alone, and never let your battery die in your car or cell.

THE VALUE OF AN OBJECTIVE PERSPECTIVE

If you are dealing with a narcissist, you may not be able to turn the tables safely. You may have to accept that you have to end the relationship and move on. If you want to preserve your relationship with someone after addressing their toxic patterns and behaviors, you need a mediator—an unbiased third party—to help restore the power balance in your relationship. Sometimes when we hear a point of view from a third party, we are more accepting of it than if the same words came from our partner.

manipulation or take actions to protect your own well-being. If your mother constantly guilt-trips you, if your sibling refuses to accept your lifestyle, if your friend spreads lies about you so she can look better, if your coworker sabotages your work so they can get promoted, if your spouse cheats on you and then blames you for their cheating, it's time to push back.

Why Is It So Hard for Some People to Say No?

We are battling some of our deepest instincts when we set a task for ourselves to create boundaries and walls between us and a human we may (or may not) care deeply about. Reasons we can't say no might be:

- We lack confidence and determination in our decisions.
- We fear absolutes and are uncomfortable with demands.
- We are still hopeful: We believe that it's still possible for the toxic person to change and become a better human.
- We are determined fixers who refuse to "give up."

Romantic Relationships and Boundaries

Romantic relationships are built on trust, vulnerability, and emotional intimacy. A manipulative partner can exploit these things to control you. When you learn to speak to a controlling partner in a way that exudes power, you can protect yourself from their overbearing presence and restore a healthier balance in your relationship.

Knowing your partner's quirks can help you customize those boundaries. Some people have short fuses and blow up over everything, while others blow up less frequently but in a bigger way. My husband likes to compare himself to a stick of dynamite (with frequent but small explosions), and me to C4 explosives (less frequent, but stronger). The best way he can diffuse tension with me is to allow me to talk openly about what bothers me. That way my anger doesn't sit and fester. For him, it's important that I don't take his little blowups so personally: He just has a shorter fuse. Our collective boundary is that no one can cross the line of respect and decency. We fight fair. We

FIVE RULES FOR PUSHING BACK

1. **Know your values:** Understand what matters to you and where you draw the line.
2. **Be assertive, not aggressive:** State your boundaries calmly and respectfully.
3. **Set realistic, achievable boundaries:** Make sure you're working toward a goal that's possible to reach.
4. **Practice saying no:** A simple "No, I'm not comfortable with that" can be incredibly powerful.
5. **Stay consistent:** Manipulators test limits. Enforcing your boundaries repeatedly sends a clear message.

can vent, complain, and get angry—that's what they do—but we can never hurt, abuse, manipulate, or deceive each other. Consider whether that boundary is there for you, and if it isn't, take steps to put it in place:

- **Recognize the manipulation tactics:** For instance, if your partner frequently tries to make you feel bad for spending time with friends, understand that this behavior is about control, not love.

- **Speak up for yourself:** Clearly state your needs using "I" statements to avoid sounding accusatory. For example: "I value my friendships, and I need time to nurture them without feeling guilty."

- **Draw the line:** Be explicit about unacceptable behavior. Say something like, "It's not OK for you to check my phone or track where I go. I need my privacy."

- **Enforce the boundary:** If they violate it, follow through. For example, if they continue the behavior, you might say, "We talked about this, and I won't tolerate it. If it happens again, I'll have to reconsider our relationship."

Family Relationships and Boundaries

Family dynamics are difficult to change because they've operated on autopilot for as long as you can remember. The people you've grown up knowing can diminish you in ways that no one else can because they know what makes you tick. Family members often rely on shared history and emotional ties to override your boundaries. By calmly asserting yourself and refusing to engage in guilt-driven tactics, you maintain control without escalating conflict. If you need tools to put what you need into words, here are some proven tactics:

- **Acknowledge their perspective without giving in:** You can empathize without agreeing. If your mom is angry that you're not coming for a visit and says, "After all I've done for you, this is how you repay me?" you can say, "I hear that you're disappointed. I want to see you, and I will plan a visit soon. Please understand that I can't change my plans this time."

- **Be honest about your limits:** Let your family member know what works for you. If it's a missed family event, you might assert yourself by saying, "I can't attend every family gathering, but I'll make an effort to come to the most important ones."

- **Anticipate and neutralize guilt:** Expect emotional appeals, but stay firm. If a family member is asking you to do too much for them, say, "I love you and appreciate you. Please understand that this responsibility is something that I can't take on. It's not something I'm able to handle right now."

- **Create space if needed:** If they continue to disregard your boundaries, consider limiting contact or setting stricter limits.

Friendships and Boundaries

Manipulative friends may exploit your kindness or expect one-sided effort. For example, they might repeatedly ask for favors or money using a line that reeks of emotional blackmail, like, "If you were a real friend, you'd do this for me."

- **Define mutual expectations:** Let them know what friendship means to you. You might say, for example, "I care about you, but I need balance in our friendship. I can't always be the one reaching out or helping."

- **Address specific behaviors:** When they push too far, call it out gently but firmly. If it's money they want from you, you could say, "I can't lend you money again. I've already helped you a lot, and I need to take care of my own finances." If they persist, follow up with: "I've already explained my boundary. I'm not going to change my mind."

- **Be ready to walk away:** If they consistently ignore your boundaries, consider whether the friendship is a positive part of your life. Tell them, "I value our friendship, but if my boundaries aren't respected, I can't continue like this." True friends will respect your boundaries. Manipulative ones will likely push back, but standing firm allows you to see their true intentions and protect your emotional well-being.

THE POWER OF POSITIVE LANGUAGE: WORDS MATTER

Negative language, telling someone they can't do something, is not as affective in changing a toxic person's behavior. No one wants to be told what they can't do; it makes them defensive. When you use positive language and tell someone they *can* do something, it's much more effective and gets people to listen.

For example, instead of saying, "You can't make that decision without my input," try saying, "When I give you my input, you can make the decision." Likewise, instead of saying, "I won't meet with you until you find a solution," you could say, "Once you find a solution, I will meet with you."

Workplace Relationships

Whether you're being overloaded with work at your job or a coworker is undermining your confidence, manipulation in a professional atmosphere seems to feed off unspoken expectations and ambiguity. Documentation and clearly drawn lines will prove invaluable when dark psychology enters the workplace. For example, a controlling boss or coworker might say, "You're the only one who can do this. If you don't help, the team will fail."

- **Set clear limits on your time:** Politely but firmly say, "I'm happy to help, but I'll need an extension on my other tasks to make this possible."
- **Document interactions:** Keep a record of requests and responses to protect yourself if things escalate.
- **Involve management or HR if necessary:** If boundaries are repeatedly crossed, escalate professionally. You might say, "I've communicated my workload clearly, but the expectations continue to be unrealistic. I'd like to discuss how we can address this."

Social Media Boundaries

In the digital age, dark psychology is free to fester. You can be harassed or trolled, you can be exposed to elaborate scams, and you can be tricked into sharing personal details or engaging in behaviors that may later come back to haunt you. The best way to put up boundaries online is to engage less. By refusing to play into a scammer's hands, you maintain control and protect your peace.

- **Limit what you share:** Draw lines when you feel like someone is trying to gather personal information about you that you don't want to share: "I prefer not to discuss my personal life online. Let's keep the conversation focused on other topics."

- **Use technology to enforce boundaries:** Mute, block, or report individuals who cross the line.

- **Disengage from manipulative behavior:** Don't respond to comments or messages designed to provoke you.

SELF-PRESERVATION AND HEALING AFTER DARK PSYCHOLOGY

If the other party cannot respect your boundaries, you need to remove them from your circle. Start with these four building blocks for establishing what you will put up with and what you won't.

1. Establish clear boundaries in your physical space. Keep them at arm's length—literally. If you need to meet with a narcissistic boss, for example, choose an open area where others are around instead of your private office or cubicle. This way, if they become defensive, controlling, accusatory, or condescending, there will be others around to witness their behavior.

2. Set your communication boundaries. Tell them that you will not tolerate aggressive, hurtful, or disrespectful communication practices from them. If they cannot treat you with respect, walk away.

3. Set your consequences for disrespectful, manipulative and abusive behavior. No is *no*. It is not up for debate. And clearly state the consequences if they do not adhere to your boundaries.

4. Keep everything documented. You may need to talk to Human Resources if this is a work relationship or a lawyer if laws have been broken, so be sure to write down every detail so that you can point to specific dates and behaviors.

Ultimately, the decision is yours to make. If you're unsure about what you can tolerate and what you cannot, consider discussing it with a close friend, a mentor, or a therapist. Many people are available to help you through this. The worst thing you can do is shut yourself off from the world and try to handle everything on your own. Very few individuals can successfully navigate such challenges alone and come out on top. Setting boundaries can feel uncomfortable at first, especially with manipulative individuals, but standing firm is the only way to step back into your power after being a victim of dark psychology.

#10 ADD SOME DISTANCE OR #11 WALK AWAY

MANIPULATORS CAN BE CUNNING. They often try to provoke you into an argument by using confusion to frustrate you. Once they identify your triggers, they can use that knowledge against you in the future to control your actions. Engaging with them continuously can lead you deeper into their trap, which is exactly what they desire. They may flip the narrative to blame you or portray themselves as the victim, leaving you in a worse situation than before. There are people who feed on hate and discontent. They are addicted to stress and anger. These individuals thrive on engagement and seek an opportunity to become belligerent and abusive. To avoid taking accountability for their anger, they will find every excuse to blame someone else for making them angry. If you engage an antagonist like this, you take the risk of feeding their fury, so ignoring the person or behavior can sometimes be a better option. The more space you can create between you and this toxic person, the better.

If required, be prepared to walk away from an antagonist or a serial manipulator as fast as you can without looking back. If you can't completely cut ties, get some healthy distance. Build a network of support to keep you from falling back into old patterns and unhealthy ties.

DETERMINING WHETHER YOU NEED TO WALK AWAY

Ask yourself the questions below to work through the process of figuring out how toxic your relationship might be and deciding whether to stay in it, take a break, or end it once and for all. You need to ask yourself:

1. WHY am I in this relationship?
2. WHAT am I getting from it?
3. HOW is it benefiting and rewarding me?
4. WHERE is this relationship going in the future?
5. DO I feel safe?

EMOTIONALLY DETACHING FROM A MANIPULATOR

Stockholm syndrome happens when victims (of abuse, kidnapping, hostage situations, and even dark psychology) develop an emotional bond with their captors or abusers and sympathetic feelings toward them. When victims have to rely on their physical or emotional captor for basic needs like safety, shelter, food, water, love, or belonging, they may begin to emotionally bond with their captors, as the captors are ensuring their survival and safety. As this bond forms, feelings of compassion and sympathy can develop. Additionally, a group mentality can emerge, creating a clear distinction between the captor and the victim on the inside, and the rest of the world on the outside. If the victims and captors are in close spaces for long periods of time, Stockholm syndrome can set in rather quickly. Studies done mostly on former POWs by Edgar Schein and Robert Lifton in the early 1960s lent evidence to the fact that prisoners could indeed have their minds and values shaped by their captor. (Slate, 2002).

Although this term tends to describe physical captors and their victims, it also applies in a similar way to emotional captors and the victims of dark psychology. When manipulators gain so much power over you and your self-esteem that you come to depend on them, it may be very difficult to find fault with them or motivate yourself to break bonds with them, especially if you no longer feel confident or secure in your own judgment and decisions.

Victims of cult leaders like Keith Raniere mentioned earlier are also prone to Stockholm syndrome because they are made to become dependent. The cult leader lures them in with charm, gifts, love, and praise, then they beat them (emotionally or physically) into submission and make it appear as though their bad behavior warranted severe punishment. Then they build their victims back up again and go back to the charm, affection, attention, and gifts. The victims become dependent on the leader to feel included, loved, and safe and may never want to leave the leader or their cult.

The bond bias can also come into play and make victims unwilling to break free from a toxic person. As discussed in Chapter 3, the bond bias makes us you feel like part of a group that's bonded by likes or dislikes, personality traits, commonalities, or experiences. When we bond with a person or group of people, we tend to trust those in the group and fear or dislike others outside the group. If someone using dark psychology can convince you that it's you and them against the world, it may take a lot of inner strength to leave that relationship.

ESCAPING A TOXIC MARRIAGE

If you have been in a long-term relationship, you may have developed deep-rooted neural pathways that take time to change. For instance, if you are in an abusive marriage and every time you mention the possibility of divorce they respond with physical aggression or verbal abuse, the idea of discussing divorce may be terrifying. As a result, you might intentionally avoid taking steps toward divorcing your partner in order to escape the anxiety it causes.

Overcoming that fear can require significant effort, but it is possible if you have determination and willpower. It's important to ask yourself if it's worth your time to attempt this change. If discussions about divorce lead to anger and irrational behavior, you may be able to work through it together. Numerous resources are available, such as camps, therapy, and counseling, that can support you both. However, if trying to leave puts you in danger of physical harm, it may be best to distance yourself from the individual. Allow them to seek the help they need first. Once they have addressed their issues, you may have the opportunity to build a new, healthy relationship with them.

THE BENEFIT OF A LITTLE DISTANCE

There is a spectrum of manipulation that ranges from lightly controlling to sadistic. When you are the victim of a psychopath, a sociopath, or someone with a personality disorder, you have a more serious issue, for which where added space or a temporary hiatus probably isn't enough of a solution. If there's someone in your life who's well-meaning but has a nasty habit of guilt-tripping, for example, some boundaries and added distance can be empowering.

BE PREPARED FOR THE FALLOUT

If you ignore or leave someone who is well-versed in dark psychology, expect them to instill guilt and fear. They will try to make you feel like you quit on them and didn't try hard enough to talk things through. Don't fall for their manipulation. Move forward with your plan and power moves.

I have a friend whose father tormented him by saying that everything my friend did was designed to hurt him. That was how his father perceived his actions. In reality, my friend tried very hard to make his father feel appreciated and loved, but nothing he did or said was ever good enough. His father found fault with every good gesture.

No one wants to abandon their parent, but my friend felt that he had no choice but to at least step away. He set boundaries and took a few months off from communicating with his father. Over time, and with some distance, he was able to figure out that the root of the issue had more to do with his father's feelings of abandonment after his divorce. He'd projected those feelings onto his son. His dad would always struggle to trust another person, fearing that they would cheat or deceive him as his ex-wife had. As a result, he clung to his son to keep him close, attempting to prevent any possibility of abandonment. They are rebuilding their relationship, but stepping away and getting space allowed both of them to work through their broken and toxic dynamic.

15

#12 GET SUPPORT AND #13 BE RESILIENT

THERE ARE ALWAYS RESOURCES to tap into for help with ending a relationship that is limiting your happiness or your confidence and growth. I wouldn't say this if I didn't prove this in my own life. Over a decade ago, I walked away from a partner and an expensive home that we'd purchased together. It wasn't an abusive relationship in any way, but I no longer wanted to be in it. I couldn't lie to myself: I wasn't in love with him. The conversation we had to have was grueling, but I knew I would survive it. After we split, I had eleven pets to care for, no job, and no money. I was living in rock bottom's basement, but I was determined to make it work. I was so confident in my decision to end our relationship that I knew what came afterward would only require my determination and will. I sought help from my family and friends, and a year later, I was living in a nice condo with all of my animals and had landed a high-paying job, a fun volunteer gig, great new friends, and a whole new life for myself. If you genuinely want a better life, particularly if you are in a toxic, demeaning, or manipulative relationship, you can have it.

WHEN THEY MAKE IT HARD TO LEAVE

First, ask yourself why this person still wants to be connected to you. Remember the story I shared about my friend Molly in Chapter 5, Love and Dark Psychology? Her ex-husband abused her, both psychically and mentally, and even years after the divorce, he refused to let her go. He would visit her in order to gather their children for the weekend and leave her love notes. To this day, this guy has never dated another woman. Why? He wanted to win Molly back, and when he couldn't he missed having total control over her. If this sounds familiar to you, you must:

1. **Set clear boundaries that will either cut all ties or allow some on specific conditions.** Maybe you tell a partner who has proven themselves to be a toxic force in your life that they can pick up the children every other weekend, but set the boundary that they cannot enter your home and must wait in your driveway.

2. **You must believe that you are in control and set conditions with authority, never bending on them.** Once they see your power, the person who once made you feel small may start to respect you. If they see you as vulnerable or weak, they will continue to try to control you.

3. **Be respectful, calm, and confident.** Being powerful is not being a tyrant. It is the exact opposite: It's saying no rather than maybe. It's deciding with conviction and seeing things through. It's communicating firmly and controlling the narrative. It's staying true to your morals and values.

WHEN YOU NEED TO CALL THE POLICE

It's always best to call an emergency crisis line, reach out to your local police, or seek legal advice if you are in danger or need information. In addition to those resources, here are some basic guidelines from a Tampa detective who has watched dozens of victims seek an escape from violent or dangerous individuals.

1. **Get a restraining order.** This can create distance from someone who is threatening or hurting you. Keep in mind, however, that a restraining order is just a piece of paper. The perpetrator might still violate the order by making contact with you.

2. **Avoid blaming yourself.** The manipulation and abuse of dark psychology are not your doing. It can be difficult to accept that your partner is fully to blame, especially if they are gaslighting you or you are still in love with them. It takes immense strength and courage to finally put an end to the emotional torment and reach out for help.

3. **Change your phone number and deactivate social media.** If the case is severe enough, you would be wise to eliminate these points of contact. Some victims even have to relocate if the subject continues to come after them.

4. **Don't drop the case.** Even if the authorities arrest the individual, most victims will drop their case by the time it gets to court. This happens a lot with domestic violence situations. It often leads to another incident when the subject becomes angry again. As the aggression intensifies, the level of violence also increases. The next time law enforcement gets involved, the victim might be hurt even more, or worse.

Once law enforcement is involved, they will assist you with the next steps to get a restraining order (or the injunction, as they call it). However, it falls heavily on you, the victim, to continue the process. You have to show up in court or the judge will drop the order. You have to be willing to pursue charges with your state attorney or district attorney or the subject will be released. If you are willing to fully pursue the charges, you are more likely to have a good outcome, with the subject receiving prison time.

BUILDING UP RESILIENCE IN THE AFTERMATH OF DARK PSYCHOLOGY

It is crucial that we don't allow manipulators and abusers to take our happiness away. It's also critical that we confront our deepest self-doubts and move forward after difficulties. Everyone has the

TRUE-CRIME CASE STUDY: SUPPORT IS A GAME-CHANGER

Without support from friends, family, religious leaders, strangers, or police, it can be very difficult to remove a dangerous person from your life. Bringing criminal charges against a domestic abuser is not an easy process, so without a source of encouragement and help from those around them, many give up and return to their abuser or manipulator.

Consider the real-life example of a man and woman in their early twenties: Let's call them Emma and Ralph. They were not married and did not live together, but they had a child together. Ralph had a history of domestic violence toward Emma and other former partners, but none of the victims followed through in the process with the courts to successfully prosecute Ralph and put an end to his violence.

Ralph was very jealous and wanted to control Emma, often telling her that he could do whatever he wanted to her because she was the mother of his kid. On the night of an incident when authorities became involved, Ralph had learned that Emma went on a date with another man. He broke into her residence at 2:00 a.m., held her down, and demanded to know who the date was. He assaulted her to impose his control over her. He then forced her into his car, drove to a convenience store, and bought Plan B for her. While at the store, Ralph argued with Emma and struck her in the face. A good Samaritan saw the interaction and intervened, helping Emma get away from him. When she returned home later, she called law enforce-

ingredients to heal after a difficult and harrowing experience with dark psychology. Even if you don't think you're the kind of person who can ever recover, it's time to shift your mindset and start believing it for your own sake and for your future.

ment. Ultimately, enough evidence was obtained to successfully arrest Ralph for the incident. Throughout the investigation, Emma needed constant encouragement to continue with the charges, because she was fearful that he would get out of jail and come after her and her child.

When Ralph was released on bail, he did attempt to contact Emma numerous times, even though there was an active restraining order against him. Authorities were eventually able to revoke his bond due to those violations, so he was sent back to jail to await trial. While the case was moving through the court system, Emma needed constant reassurance and support to continue with it. She was scared, nervous, and worried about what Ralph might do if he was found not guilty.

After several months of talks and help from a victim's advocate, Emma agreed to testify at the jury trial against Ralph. On the day of the trial, she was terrified and emotional but still mustered up the courage to take the stand while he looked on. In the end, thanks to her bravery and the commitment of her supporters, he was found guilty of two out of three counts and was sentenced to twenty years in prison. After the trial, Emma tearfully thanked everyone involved for giving her the strength to finally move forward with the case. She stated that she never received as much support with the domestic violence calls she'd made in the past and that she was grateful she finally received it. The process was finally over and she and her child were safe.

There are four types of resilience that are inherent in everyone:

1. Physical resilience: This is when a sick person rapidly recovers from illness.

2. Mental resilience: This happens when your own hate, stress, and anxiety are replaced by love, acceptance, and peace. It happens when negative thoughts and depression give way to energy and motivation.

3. Emotional resilience: This is when you accept your emotions, can express them without fear, and discover self-acceptance.

4. Social resilience: This kind of resilience manifests as showing up in the world again with your friends and family, going back to work, and putting yourself "out there."

STEPS TO RESILIENCE

There are four steps that can help you move forward after you've been a victim of dark psychology and manipulation.

Step 1: Cope now. Even in the toughest of times, you must fight your negative feelings rather than succumb to them. They cannot win and take over your well-being. Start right now. Be optimistic and grateful for the lessons your experience has taught you. To help you do that, consider or write down the answers to these questions. Forcing yourself to write five answers pushes you to really think about them.

- Having been through a traumatic experience, how might it have been worse?

- What are the lessons you learned from this experience that will help you protect yourself in the future?

- What are five things you are grateful for right now?

- How can you use your experience to help others: Your family, friends, or colleagues?

Step 2: Use your support. Remember that you don't have to go it alone! You are surrounded by people who would be happy to lend a helping hand, offer advice, or listen. Let them help you. By letting them help you, you make them feel good about themselves. It's a win-win situation! List five people you can count on who will be there for you and who want to help you.

Step 3: Cultivate mindfulness. Mindfulness is the process of bringing our attention to the internal and external experiences happening in and around us at the present moment. Author, professor, and mindfulness teacher Jon Kabat-Zinn describes it as "the awareness that emerges through paying attention on purpose, in the present moment, and nonjudgmentally, to the unfolding of experience moment by moment." Mindfulness practices help us increases awareness about our feelings, emotions, senses, thoughts, reactions, decisions, verbal and nonverbal language, and even intuition or gut feelings.

When we become more aware, we are less likely to ruminate on the past or worry about the future. Worry and rumination can both contribute to depression and anxiety, which can produce a domino effect of adverse outcomes. Mindfulness practices intervene by refocusing one's attention on the here and now. Over time, mindfulness can bring about a greater sense of well-being by improving our overall mental and physical health. It has been known to reduce stress and impulsive behaviors, and to promote togetherness, kindness, and respect and discourage negative emotions, disrespect, and confrontation.

Physiologically, mindfulness can reduce cortisol in your body, strengthen your hippocampus—the area of the brain that controls memory and learning—lower blood pressure, and improve your immune system. It creates new neuropathways (from your new mindful thoughts and behaviors) that can increase your concentration and empathy.

Its benefits are so clear that the Navy Seals, the Seattle Seahawks, Google, and Apple have all embraced mindfulness practices for their organizations. Try it out for yourself. Here are five mindfulness techniques you can start using immediately to calm your mind, lower your stress and anxiety, and open your heart to receiving and giving love and kindness after an experience with dark psychology in its many forms.

1. Breathe. Calm your nervous system by breathing properly from your diaphragm, and concentrate only on your

MINDFULNESS AND POSITIVE RENEWAL

According to a 2015 article in *Harvard Business Review* called "Mindfulness Can Literally Change Your Brain," authors Christina Congleton, Britta K. Hölzel, and Sara W. Lazar describe how mindfulness can help us heal from toxic stress and can actually increase the density of the gray matter in our brains. In a 2011 study, participants who completed an eight-week mindfulness program showed increased gray matter in the hippocampus region of the brain, which is tied to resilience and memory. While this area can be damaged by chronic stress, mindfulness appears to have the ability to restore and rebuild it.

breathing, not worrying. As you do this, you are increasing your lung capacity, improving blood oxygen levels, reducing blood pressure, and relaxing yourself. You can use what is called the 4-7-8 breath or the box breath. The 4-7-8 breath means you breathe in for a count of four, hold the breath for a count of seven, and exhale for a count of eight. Rarely do we breathe to fill our lungs and exhale all of the breath out, but when we do it helps us feel calm. Box breathing is when you inhale for a count of four, then exhale for a count of four, and repeat that sequence.

2. Kindness. Every day, wish someone kindness. It can be a friend, your spouse, or a stranger. When you train your brain to think kind thoughts, you become more empathetic. Wishing kindness makes us happier and more compassionate. The more you practice, the more your kindness will grow, and the more it will show on the outside to others. When we express kindness to others, many (not all) will be more likely to reciprocate it.

3. Practice an attitude of gratitude. Gratitude makes us happy. When I am grateful, wonderful things happen to me. My happiness and gratitude are attracting that same energy in the universe and repelling negative energy. That's why I always receive good news and fortune when I am happy and grateful, and never when I'm angry, sad, or complaining.

4. Work on your inner critic. You are your best advocate, protector, and cheerleader. Rely on yourself to lift you up before you rely on others. You won't fail yourself, but others may. You must love, trust, nurture, and be patient with yourself. Give yourself kindness and show yourself grace. If you treat yourself poorly or think little of yourself, others may feel free to do the same.

Your inner critic will tell you that you're not good enough, not smart enough, not attractive enough, and not worthy. When you hear your inner critic's thoughts, tell them to shut up. Say it out loud if you have to. They are sabotaging your inner advocate, but don't let them! If you trusted someone you shouldn't have, don't beat yourself up. Do better next time. Learn from your mistakes, because we all make them. Instead, take part in activities to kick out the inner critic and praise the inner advocate:

a. When you're going through a difficult time, it's helpful to ask your close family and friends what they appreciate and love about you, then do the same for them.

b. Each morning, start with an attention activity. Take a few minutes for yourself, close your eyes, and bring your attention to your inner advocate: What is it saying to you today that makes you feel loved, special, and invincible? Listen to that voice, embrace and believe it. Imagine how wonderful it would feel to start the day feeling grateful, valued, and confident.

Step 4: Bounce forward. I don't like to say bounce back. I like to keep moving forward and growing upward. It's OK to take a few minutes with your emotions and be angry, sad, and hurt. But then, bounce forward! Don't dwell on the past; focus on the future. Stop thinking about what you cannot change. Start thinking about what you can change. Rise to the challenge and come back stronger.

AVOID BECOMING ANOTHER VICTIM: FIGHT BACK WITH THE 13 POWER MOVES

Even as I was writing this book, I discovered that another person in my life was a victim of cleverly hidden manipulation. The deception was so covertly executed that she was married to him for years before she knew the truth behind his dark games. Here is how dark psychology played out in her life, in her words:

"It's difficult to find the right words after everything I've endured, but it's time to reveal the truth. I was married to a man who masqueraded as a respected veteran: kind, loving, and honest. Yet beneath that façade was a deceitful, manipulative narcissist. His betrayal extended far beyond his infidelity. He embezzled money, adding to the loss of my businesses, my career, and my home. He pursued sugar babies, had secretive relationships, sent cryptocurrency, and borrowed from anyone he could".

"He disowned his children, his grandchildren, and our beloved pets. Now I'm left to pick up the pieces of a shattered life. To my children, grandson, and everyone who has supported me, thank you for your love and light. I am reclaiming my power and moving forward with dignity. The road ahead may be long, but life is already feeling so much sweeter. I can't wait for my next chapter!"

I sincerely hope that this book gives you useful weapons to arm yourself against abuse and manipulation from those closest to you, and that you emerge determined and ready to move on with dignity as my friend has. If you have been a victim of dark psychology, abuse, or manipulation, or are in a relationship right now wondering whether you are, you are not alone, and you never will be. Millions of people suffer through these relationships, and most of them are able to bounce forward like the friend above. Whether or not you are a victim, the 13 Power Moves will help you learn to identify deception and overcome it. Plenty of people who encounter dark psychology have the courage to love and live again, and they go on to pursue their dreams. You can, too. You don't deserve the damage that dark psychology causes. You deserve the best life has to offer. Never forget that.

VICTIM RESOURCES

NATIONAL DOMESTIC VIOLENCE HOTLINE

1 (800) 799-7233 or Text START to 88788

WOMENSLAW EMAIL HOTLINE

hotline.womenslaw.org

SUBSTANCE ABUSE AND MENTAL HEALTH SERVICES ADMINISTRATION (SAMHSA) HELPLINE

1 (800) 662–4357

If you aren't sure which helpline is best, or if you have concerns in more than one area, contact:

THE VICTIMCONNECT RESOURCE CENTER

1-855-4VICTIM (855-484-2846)

ACKNOWLEDGMENTS

I am honored to write this book, and I couldn't have done it without the support of several individuals and organizations. First and foremost, I want to extend a very special thank you to my senior editor, Aimee Chase. Aimee, you truly had your work cut out for you. I was genuinely impressed by your edits and suggestions. Without you, this book would not have come to fruition. Thank you for partnering with me in this endeavor. Saying that I couldn't have done it without you is an understatement. I am incredibly grateful for your hard work and talent. I would love the opportunity to collaborate again in the future— if you'll have me. I appreciate everything you did to help me share this work with those who need it.

I also want to thank Spot Gloss Media, formerly Hollan Publishing—specifically Holly Schmidt who found me. I'm not sure how you did, but I am thankful. Thank you for believing in and trusting me. I am grateful.

To my friend and colleague, Robin Dreeke: I want to express my deepest gratitude for your friendship, wise words, curiosity, and especially for writing the exceptionally impactful foreword. I am continually impressed by your talent, expertise, and modesty. I am honored and truly grateful for our unbreakable alliance.

The heart of this book would not be as powerful without the real, intimate stories shared by some incredibly strong and resilient women I know personally. Thank you for being vulnerable and sharing your experiences of abuse, which will help other women learn and grow. Your courage allows them to reevaluate their relationships and make wiser, safer decisions about whom they can trust. Thank you for this invaluable gift you are offering others. I am grateful for you and honored to know you.

Kristin, thank you for your contributions to this book. The things you witness on a daily basis are shocking and appalling, yet you continue to go to work every day with a determination to make the world a better place. I am incredibly grateful that you were in my class years ago and that we have stayed connected. Your talent and commitment to continuous learning have truly impressed me. Thank you for your service to this country and for risking your life daily. You are truly a remarkable woman.

Joanna, I am so happy we met years ago. You are a true gem. Thank you so much for the work you do helping so many of us "dethrone our inner critic." We all can use your lessons.

I want to thank my husband for his contribution but more importantly for his wisdom, insights, support, and unconditional love. Partnership is never all roses, but we handle the thorns because we truly are the most effective team.

Finally, I want to thank my family—all the time and every time. I have two brothers who I would do anything for and vice versa. They drive me nuts at times, but they are my best friends. My parents—who are still married after 53 years— provided all of us a safe and loving environment. They set my moral compass, and they were always there for me in every way possible. I am truly the luckiest girl in the world to have this family.

I smiled as I finished reading the final proof because I know that this book will help someone out there to be safe and to be respected and loved. And that makes me very happy. My life's mission has transformed over the years and has become this: to teach people everything I know about human behavior—how to build trust, how to communicate confidently and wisely, and how to find the truth so that they can use what I know in their life to be successful and safe.

SOURCES

Congleton, Christina, Britta K. Hölzel, and Sara W. Lazar. "Mindfulness Can Literally Change Your Brain." Harvard Business Review. January 8, 2015. https://hbr.org/2015/01/mindfulness-can-literally-change-your-brain

Carney, D. R., Cuddy, A. J., and Yap, A. J. (2010). "Power posing: brief non-verbal displays affect neuroendocrine levels and risk tolerance." Psychological Science, 21(10), 1363–1368. https://doi.org/10.1177/0956797610383437

"Cycling's Greatest Fraud: Lance Armstrong." Peacock Productions for National Geographic Channels, June 23, 2013.

"Ex-Cop to Missing Wife: 'Make Yourself Seen," ABC News. November 20, 2007. https://abcnews.go.com/GMA/story?id=3890584&page=1

Forward, Susan. Toxic Parents, Bantam Books, 2009.

"Gaslighting: The 'perfect' romance that became a nightmare." BBC News. November 28, 2017. https://www.bbc.com/news/stories-41915425

Goodchild, Joan. "Protect Your Company from Social Engineering." ComputerWorld.com. January 11, 2010. https://www.computerworld.com/article/1559457/protect-your-company-from-social-engineering.html

Grèzes, J., S. Berthoz, R.E. Passingham. "Amygdala Activation When One is the Target of Deceit: Did He Lie to You or to Someone Else?" NeuroImage, Volume 30, Issue 2 (2006): 601-608. https://doi.org/10.1016/j.neuroimage.2005.09.038.

Kleinman, Joanna. Dethroning Your Inner Critic, Un-Settling Books, 2020.

McBride, Karyl, Ph.D., Will I Ever Be Good Enough? Atria Books, 2009.

"O. J. Simpson: The Interview." H & K Productions. 1996. https://www.youtube.com/watch?v=779HhorMniE

"Pastor: Wife 'Feared' Cop Husband." CBS News. November 30, 2007. https://www.cbsnews.com/news/pastor-wife-feared-cop-husband/

Peterson, Drew. Interview by Larry King. "Drew Peterson Answers Questions." CNN Interview. April 11, 2008. https://transcripts.cnn.com/show/lkl/date/2008-04-11/segment/01

Stern, Robin, Ph.D., The Gaslight Effect, How to Spot and Survive the Hidden Manipulation Others Use to Control Your Life, Dr. Robin Stern, Forward by

Naomi Wolf. https://www.amazon.com/Gaslight-Effect-Survive-Manipulation-Control-ebook/dp/B000QCQ8X0?&_encoding=UTF8&tag=robinstern10-20&linkCode=ur2&linkId=0fa2c20b679bb2cbccd2d255982c0e5c&camp=1789&creative=9325

The Lead with Jake Tapper, CNN: New England Patriots Quarterback News Conference: January 22, 2015. https://www.youtube.com/watch?v=hXT8h1_YrsM

Villar, Gina, Joanne Arciuli, and Helen Paterson. "Vocal Pitch Production During Lying: Beliefs about Deception Matter." Psychiatry, Psychology and Law 20, Issue 1 (2012): 123–32. https://www.tandfonline.com/doi/abs/10.1080/13218719.2011.633320

Walsh, Savannah. "I Was in a Cult for 10 Years." *Vanity Fair*. October 23, 2024. www.vanityfair.com/hollywood/story/bethany-joy-lenz-book-dinner-for-vampires-one-tree-hill-cult-interview